# The Ending of Mark's Gospel

## The Key to Understanding the Gospels and Christianity

*Second Edition*

by

## Peter E. Lewis
BD Hons (Lond.), GDipTheol (BCT), MB, BS (Qld),
DTM&H (Syd.), FRCS (Eng.), FRACS

THE ENDING OF MARK'S GOSPEL:
THE KEY TO UNDERSTANDING THE GOSPELS AND CHRISTIANITY
Copyright © PETER E. LEWIS 2020

First published by Zeus Publications 2019
Second edition published by Zeus Publications 2020
http://www.zeus-publications.com
P.O. Box 2554
Burleigh M.D.C.
QLD 4220
Australia.

 A catalogue record for this book is available from the National Library of Australia

All Rights Reserved

No part of this book may be reproduced in any form, by photocopying or by any electronic or mechanical means, including information storage or retrieval systems, without permission in writing from both the copyright owner and the publisher of this book.

This book is a work of non-fiction.

The author asserts his moral rights.

ISBN: 978-1-876697-22-8

© Cover Design—Zeus Publications 2020

This book deals with Mark's gospel and in particular with why it has an abrupt ending. A rational investigation of the matter reveals that various influences were involved and that it can be the key to understanding how the gospels came to be the way they are. The gospels, of course, are integral to Christianity and hopefully this new perspective and fresh critical approach will revitalise the faith. Sadly in the Western world today Christianity is in decline and the number of people regularly attending the mainstream churches has dropped markedly in recent decades. If widely read this book could reverse that trend.

# Dedication

*For Jim, Vanessa, Suzanne and Stephen*

# Contents

Introduction................................................................1
Key texts in English and Greek:
   (a) The Abrupt Ending of Mark's Gospel...............................9
   (b) The Shorter Ending of Mark's Gospel..............................10
   (c) The Longer Ending of Mark's Gospel...............................11
   (d) The Beginning of Mark's Gospel...................................16
An Explanation for the Abrupt Ending of Mark's Gospel..................18
Bibliography...........................................................46
The Significance of the Missing Beginning and Disregarded..............51
Ending of Mark's Gospel
A New Appraisal of Mark's Gospel.......................................76
A Theological Reflection on the Ending of Mark's Gospel................82
The Denarius n Mark 12:15..............................................88
Afterword..............................................................124

# Introduction

In this book there are five articles. Although they are all about Mark's gospel the last article, 'The Denarius in Mark 12:15', deals with only one verse and focuses on ancient coins, but I have included it because it explains how I got started on this intellectual journey which has given me a particular understanding of the gospels and Christianity. I now feel that I should share my insights with others, hence this book.

I am not a clergyman. Nor am I a professional biblical scholar. I am a retired surgeon, but I have always had a strong Christian faith and since I was in my 20s (I am 80 now) I have taken an interest in the academic side of Christianity. My early part-time studies in religion at the University of Queensland were cut short when I went as a volunteer surgeon to Bangladesh for three years. That was in the 1970s after the terrible war for the independence of Bangladesh. Then when I was the surgeon for the Solomon Islands (where there was no television to watch at night) I gained an honours degree in divinity from London University by correspondence. When I returned to Queensland I was a GP until I retired from medical practice in 2002 although I continued in a non-clinical capacity as the vice-president of Hopewell Hospice on the Gold Coast. During this time I studied part-time at the

Brisbane College of Theology eventually obtaining a postgraduate diploma in Theology. I had studied Greek at a postgraduate level and was able to read the New Testament in the language in which it was originally written. Having done Latin at the Brisbane State High School (where I was the dux), I was well equipped to undertake research in an independent way which would not have been possible if I was a priest or minister of religion. Even if I had been a professional biblical scholar working in a university or seminary I would have been constrained by all sorts of influences because 'rocking the boat' could lead to unemployment.

I have always had a strong Christian faith. I regularly attend the local church where I enjoy worshipping God in a formal way and where I am grateful for the spiritual boost that I receive and for the Christian fellowship. As none of my relatives are churchgoers I have often wondered why this is so important to me, whereas they couldn't care less. I realise it is just who I am, which means it is part of my genetic make-up. In recent years some geneticists have suggested that religious people have a 'God gene'. In other words there is something in their DNA which gives them an innate awareness that there is more than just the material world and it directs them to believe in God. This is very much the case with me, and being rather introverted I take what would be considered a mystical approach. When I wake in the morning and see the dawn, when I look at the ocean during the day, and when I see the stars at night, I think of God and the wonder of it all. I am like a small child who holds a leaf in his hand for the first time.

But what affects me even more than the wonders of creation is the mystery of existence. Just being alive is impossible to comprehend. I find it amazing that I exist at all, that I am me! And I believe that life comes from God. When confronted by this phenomenon of the individuality of consciousness I cannot understand why others do not fall down and worship God. The German theologian, Rudolf Otto, was thinking along these lines when he wrote about the *Mysterium Tremendum,* the tremendous mystery of existence.

I have explained all this about my Christian faith because I want to reassure you that I am not going to destroy your belief in God or attack the Trinity or cause you to deny that Jesus was both human and divine. On the contrary, I am confident that after carefully reading this book with an open mind your Christian faith will be strengthened. It will, however, be changed in some ways because unnecessary burdens and obstacles will have been removed and you should have a fresh understanding of what life is all about. You might be shocked by some of the statements that are made, but like a rose bush it is necessary to cut off dead branches and prune it back to essentials. Only then can new growth occur and gorgeous roses blossom. In using the pruning shears I have followed where truth has led me. As Jesus said, "I am the way, the truth and the life."

Because I have made truth my guide on this path of clarification, the first two papers have been written in an academic style, i.e. there are footnotes, and evidence is given for every step in the argument. I did not want it to be just a matter of personal opinion and speculation, as so many books about Christianity are today. There is, of course, always a degree of speculation in any form of research, but I have tried to keep it to a minimum. Of course, you may not agree with all the details but I hope you will find the overall picture compelling. It will be rather like a jigsaw puzzle which you only really see when it has been completed. Although it is written in an academic style I have tried to write as clearly and simply as possible, and where there are Greek words they have been translated. It will not be an easy read because complex matters have to be explained and understood but nothing valuable is ever gained without effort.

The gist of my thesis is that by looking critically at the beginning and end of Mark's gospel one will gain knowledge of how the gospels came to be the way they are. Consequently a fundamentalist understanding of the Bible will be untenable. In the past the fundamentalist view that every word in the Bible was true resulted in such disasters as the perpetuation of slavery and flat-earth cosmology. Modern Christians must move beyond this way of thinking if Christianity is to survive into the future. Hopefully the ideas put forward in this book will initiate a new Reformation, a fresh look at what Christianity is all about. It will still be based on the Bible but in a rational way that includes these new insights. A new Reformation is greatly needed in the Western world because secularism is on the rise and overall church attendances are declining. Like my relatives, more and more people couldn't care less.

Read the first and second articles in this book in that order. The last article, about the denarius, is not as important and need not be read if time is limited. I have included it because it was the way that this whole area of biblical research was opened up for me. My hobby for many years has been collecting and studying ancient coins, and I have focused on coins relating to the history of Christianity. I have written books and many articles on the subject, and when I thought about the denarius in Mark 12:15 I realised that it could not be a denarius and it made me look critically at other passages in Mark's gospel, especially the beginning and the end where the abrupt ending has been a major problem for biblical scholars in modern times. The coin in Mark 12:15 could not be a denarius for several reasons, the chief one being that denarii did not circulate in Judaea at that time. After considering which coin was the one actually shown to Jesus it became obvious that it was a silver coin that was minted in Antioch by the emperor Tiberius.

On the coin was the claim that his predecessor, the emperor Augustus, was a god. The Jews must have shown it to Jesus to get his reaction. It revealed to me a whole new scenario behind the written text.

There was another important aspect to my numismatic studies. I was impressed by how often Heracles (Hercules to the Romans) appeared on ancient coins. From 126 BCE to 66 CE he appeared on all the silver coins minted at Tyre, which was the main commercial centre in the region. He appeared on all the silver coins issued in the name of Alexander the Great during his lifetime and for many years after his death. Actually Heracles had appeared frequently on coins ever since they were invented in the $7^{th}$ century BCE, and this showed me how popular he and the other Greek heroes were in ancient times, but unlike Superman and the other modern superheroes Heracles and the like were incorporated into the prevailing religion and mythology. A common feature of these ancient superheroes was that they were conceived by the intercourse of a god with a mortal woman. So when the Christian gospel was first preached to the Gentiles they would have anticipated that Jesus was conceived in the same way.

Mark, who was the first to write a gospel and whose work was largely copied by Luke and Matthew, did not believe that Jesus was conceived in the same way as Heracles. For Mark, Jesus was born naturally. For some readers this will be the most shocking revelation in this book, but as Bishop Spong wrote in his book *Born of a Woman* the virgin of a literal Bible, the virgin of the annunciation 'will have to go'. I agree. The doctrine of the virginal conception of Jesus is an unnecessary burden on faith. In an article entitled *The Coming Radical Reformation* Robert Funk wrote: 'The virgin birth of Jesus is an insult to modern intelligence and should be abandoned.' But conservative Christians should not despair: Jesus can still be the Son of God even though he was born naturally.

Christianity needs to get rid of the Virgin Mary if it is to be acceptable to future generations. Of course, Christians should still honour Mary as the mother of Jesus, but unfortunately during the Middle Ages (especially in the overheated religiosity of the Byzantine Empire) the situation got out of hand with Mary becoming the Queen of Heaven and the one to whom Christians should pray. The cult of Mary with the Christ child derived largely from Egyptian religion where Isis and her son Horus were worshiped with great devotion, and coins of ancient Egypt show them as they are portrayed on Christian icons.

There are other aspects of conservative Christianity which will need to be reassessed after reading this book. For example, does one need to believe in the bodily resurrection of Jesus to be a Christian? Admittedly the form that Jesus might have taken after his resurrection is beyond human comprehension. It belongs to the realm of the supernatural, but in thinking about these matters one needs to follow the path of truth as far as possible and on this path one should be accompanied by Reason.

On the Christian quest for truth it is important not to deny the supernatural. Otherwise Christianity is reduced to an ethical code or a secular philosophy. For Christians it is much more than that. They must be constantly aware of the spiritual aspect of their lives. Then life becomes really exciting and positive. They become co-creators with God in the amazing adventure to transform the cosmos and establish the Kingdom of God.

* * * * *

# The Abrupt Ending of Mark's Gospel

## Verse 16:8

So they went out and fled from the tomb, for terror and amazement had seized them; and they said nothing to anyone, for they were afraid. (NRSV)

## Greek Text

Και ἐξελθουσαι ἐφυγον ἀπο του μνημειου, εἰχεν γαρ
And going forth they fled from the tomb, it was having for

αὐτας τρομος και ἐκστασις· και οὐδενι οὐδεν εἰπαν·
them trembling and bewilderment; and to no one nothing they told;

ἐφοβουντο γαρ.
they were afraid for.

*Note: These key texts are reproduced here to save the reader referring to other books. In the ancient Greek manuscripts the words are written in capital letters with no spaces between the words.*

# The Shorter Ending of Mark's Gospel

But to those around Peter they reported concisely all that they had been commanded. And afterward Jesus himself sent out through them, from east to west, the sacred and imperishable proclamation of eternal salvation. Amen

## Greek Text

**Παντα δε τα παρηγγελμενα τοις περι τον Πετον συντομως**
all things But the ones commanded to them around the Peter concisely

**ἐξηγγειλαν. Μετα δε ταυτα και αὐτος ὁ Ἰησους ἀπο ἀνατολης**
they reported. after And these things even himself the Jesus from east

**και ἀχρι δυσεως ἐξαπεστειλεν δι' αὐτων το ἱερον και ἀφθαρτον**
and as far as west he sent out through them the sacred and imperishable

**κηρυγμα της αἰωνιου σωτηριας. Ἀμην**
proclamation of the eternal salvation. Amen

\* \* \* \* \*

# The Longer Ending of Mark's Gospel

**16:9** Now after he rose early on the first day of the week, he appeared first to Mary Magdalene, from whom he had cast out seven demons. **10** She went out and told those who had been with him, while they were mourning and weeping. **11** But when they heard that he was alive and had been seen by her, they would not believe it. **12** After this he appeared in another form to two of them, as they were walking into the country. **13** And they went back and told the rest, but they did not believe them. **14** Later he appeared to the eleven themselves as they were sitting at the table; and he upbraided them for their lack of faith and stubbornness, because they had not believed those who saw him after he had risen. **15** And he said to them, "Go into all the world and proclaim the good news to the whole creation. **16** The one who believes and is baptised will be saved; but the one who does not believe will be condemned. **17** And these signs will accompany those who believe: by using my name they will cast out demons; they will speak in new tongues; **18** they will pick up snakes in their hands, and if they drink any deadly thing, it will not hurt them; they will lay their hands on the sick, and they will recover." **19** So then the Lord Jesus, after he had spoken to them was taken up into heaven and sat down at the right hand of God. **20** And they went out and proclaimed the good news everywhere, while the Lord worked with them and confirmed the message by the signs that accompanied it. (NRSV)

## Greek Text

**9** Ἀναστας δε πρωι πρωτῃ σαββατου ἐφανη πρωτον Μαριᾳ τῃ
rising But early on first of week he appeared first to Mary the

Μαγδαληνῃ, παρ' ἡς ἐκβεβληκει ἐπτα δαιμονια. **10** ἐκεινη πορευθεισα
Magdalene, from whom he had expelled seven demons. She going

ἀπηγγειλεν τοις μετ' αὐτου γενομενοις πενθουσι και κλαιουσιν·
reported to the ones with him having been mourning and weeping;

**11** κἀκεινοι ἀκουσαντες ὁτι ζῃ και ἐθεαθη ὑπ' αὐτης ἠπιστησαν.
and those hearing that he lives and was seen by her disbelieved.

**12** Μετα δε ταυτα δυσιν ἐξ αὐτων περιπατουσιν ἐφανερωθη ἐν
after And these things to two of them walking he was manifested in

ἑτέρᾳ μορφῇ πορευομενοις εἰς ἀγρον· 13 κἀκεινοι ἀπελθοντες ἀπηγγειλαν
different form travelling into country; and those going reported

τοις λοιποις· οὐδε ἐκεινοις ἐπιστευσαν. 14 Ὕστερον ἀνακειμενοις αὐτοις
to the rest; not them they believed. Later to the reclining them

τοις ἐνδεκα ἐφανερωθη και ὠνειδισεν την ἀπιστιαν αὐτων και
the eleven he was manifested and he reproached the disbelief of them and

σκληροκαρδιαν ὅτι τοις θεασαμενοις αὐτον ἐγηγερμενον οὐκ
hardness of heart because the ones beholding him having been raised not

ἐπιστευσαν. 15 και εἰπεν αὐτοις· πορευθεντες εἰς τον κοσμον ἁπαντα
believed. And he said to them: Going into the world all

κηρυξατε το εὐαγγελιον πασῃ τῃ κτισει. 16 ὁ πιστευσας και
proclaim the good news to all the creation. The one believing and

βαπτισθεις σωθησεται, ὁ δε ἀπιστησας κατακριθησεται. 17 σημεια
being baptised will be saved, the one but disbelieving will be condemned. signs

δε τοις πιστευσασιν ταυτα παρακολουθησει· ἐν τῷ ὀνοματι μου
And the ones believing these will follow; in the name of me

δαιμονια ἐκβαλουσιν, γλωσσαις λαλησουσιν καιναις, 18 ὀφεις ἀρουσιν
demons they will expel, with tongues they will speak new, snakes they will take

κἀν θανασιμον τι πιωσιν οὐ μη αὐτους βλαψῃ, ἐπι ἀρρωστους
and if deadly anything they drink by no means them it will hurt, on sick ones

χειρας ἐπιθησουσιν και καλως ἑξουσιν. 19 Ὁ μεν οὖν κυριος μετα
hands they will place and well they will have. The therefore Lord after

το λαλησαι αὐτοις ἀνελημφθη εἰς τον οὐρανον και ἐκαθισεν ἐκ
the to speak to them he was taken up into the heaven and sat at

δεξιων του θεου. 20 ἐκεινοι δε ἐξελθοντες ἐκηρυξαν πανταχου,
right hand of God. those But going forth proclaimed everywhere,

του κυριου συνεργουντος και τον λογον βεβαιουντος δια των
the Lord working with and the word confirming through the

**ἐπακολουθουντων σημειων.**

accompanying signs.

\* \* \* \* \*

# The Beginning of Mark's Gospel

**1:1** The beginning of the gospel about Jesus Christ, the Son of God.

**2** As it is written in the prophet Isaiah,

"See I am sending my messenger ahead of you

who will prepare your way;

**3** the voice of one crying out in the wilderness:

'Prepare the way of the Lord, make his paths straight'."

**4** John the baptiser appeared in the wilderness, proclaiming a baptism of repentance for the forgiveness of sins.

## Greek Text

**1** Ἀρχη του εὐαγγελιου Ἰησου Χριστου Υἱου Θεου.

Beginning of the gospel of Jesus Christ Son of God.[1]

**2** Καθως γεγραπται ἐν τῳ Ἡσαιᾳ τῳ προφητῃ·

Just as it has been written in the Isaiah the prophet:

---

[1] In the New International Version, the New Jerusalem Bible and the Good News Bible, Mark 1:1 is translated as: The beginning of the gospel about Jesus Christ, the Son of God.

ἰδου ἀποστελλω τον ἀγγελον μου προ προσωπου σου,
Behold I send the messenger of me before face of you,
ὁς κατασκευασει την ὁδον σου·
who will prepare the way of you;

3 φωνη βοωντος ἐν τῃ ἐρημῳ· ἐτοιμασατε την ὁδον κυριου,
a voice of crying in the desert: 'Prepare the way of Lord

εὐθειας ποιειτε τας τριβους αὐτου,
straight make the paths of him,'

4 ἐγενετο Ἰωαννης ὁ βαπτιζων ἐν τῃ ἐρημῳ κηρυσσων
so appeared John the one baptising in the desert proclaiming

βαπτισμα μετανοιας εἰς ἀφεσιν ἁμαρτιων.
a baptism of repentance for forgiveness of sins.

\* \* \* \* \*

# An Explanation for the Abrupt Ending of Mark's Gospel

**Abstract**

In some ancient manuscripts Mark's gospel ends abruptly with ἐφοβοῦντο γάρ (for they were afraid), but others have in addition a short or long ending or both. A new explanation is proposed. The whole outer leaf of the gospel was deliberately removed, thus removing the beginning and end of the gospel. The likely reason was that the disciples were portrayed as stubbornly not believing that Jesus had risen and Mark had described Jesus's birth as natural, which was unacceptable to the Gentile Christians in Rome. In some cases the original last page was added to subsequent copies, and this explains the various combinations of endings.

\* \* \* \* \*

*Note: The reader will find it helpful to refer to the diagram on page 45.*

The gospel attributed to Mark is the shortest of the canonical gospels and there are features which suggest that part of it is missing. Although it is generally considered to be the earliest gospel the date of its writing is disputed by scholars. For the purposes of the argument presented here it will be assumed that it was the first gospel and that it was written at an early date in Rome. Rome is the most likely provenance given the strength of the early tradition and the fact that in the pericope about the widow's offering (Mark 12.41-44) the author explains to the readers that her two small coins were worth a quadrans, which was a coin that circulated only in Italy. Moreover, the fact that Jewish customs are explained in Mark 7.3 indicates that the author expected that at least some of the readers would be Gentiles.

The literature concerning the ending of Mark's gospel is vast, and to engage in conversation with modern scholars in all aspects of the problem would inordinately expand the scope of this article, the purpose of which is to concisely present a new explanation for the abrupt ending of Mark's gospel. It will be argued that Mark had written about the parentage and birth of Jesus but this information was on the first page which was removed when someone pulled off the outer leaf of the codex, thus removing the first and last pages of the gospel. Moreover, it will be explained how the original ending of the gospel seamlessly followed on from Mark 16.8. The original ending is reconstructed and shown to be an appropriate ending to the gospel.

Although some modern New Testament scholars[2] consider Mark's gospel to be complete as it is, for others[3] it is inconceivable that he would end his gospel with the statement that when the women found the tomb empty: 'They said nothing to anyone, for they were afraid'. (Mark 16.8) Also the final word in the Greek text is γάρ (for), which is unexpected at the end of a Greek manuscript. According to Michael J. Kok, 'A minority of scholars cannot fathom that Mark originally terminated at 16:8 and assume that damage to the manuscript resulted in a lost ending'.[4]

Mark's gospel ends at 16.8 in two ancient manuscripts, Codex Sinaiticus and Codex Vaticanus (both from the 4th century), and Eusebius[5] and Jerome[6] both state that there was nothing more in most of the manuscripts available to them. The 4th-century Sinaitic Syriac version also ends at 16.8 as does the 12th-century manuscript 304. In the other extant manuscripts, however, there is

---

[2] For example, Daniel B. Wallace, 'Mark 16:8 as the Conclusion to the Second Gospel', *Perspectives on the Ending of Mark* (ed. D. A. Black; Nashville: Broadman & Holman, 2008), 1-39.

[3] N.T. Wright considers that the opening and closing of the original are lost. He wrote: 'I tried for some years to believe that Mark was really a postmodernist who would deliberately leave his gospel with a dark and puzzling ending, but I have for some time now given up the attempt. . . it could not have ended without the story of the risen, vindicated Jesus.' ('The Resurrection of the Messiah', *TRev* 41.2 (1998) 107-56, at 136).

[4] M. J. Kok, *The Gospel on the Margins: The Reception of Mark in the 2nd century* (Minneapolis: Fortress Press, 2015) 42.

[5] Eusebius, *Ad Marinus*, in *Nova Patrum Bibliotheca* 4, 255.

[6] Jerome, *Letter to Hedibria*, in *Epistola 120, Patrologia Latina*, 22.986-87.

an additional short ending[7] or long ending[8] or both.[9] In those manuscripts with both endings the shorter ending always precedes the longer ending.

Some modern scholars believe that the longer ending is what Mark originally wrote.[10] They point to the patristic citations of the longer ending as early as the 2nd century.[11] Scholars who find an ending at 16.8 incredible have suggested that the last page of the gospel is missing. Bruce Metzger considered it most probable that 'the Gospel accidentally lost its last leaf before it was multiplied

---

[7] Only the Old Latin MS, Codex Bobiensis (k), has just the short ending. It has been dated to c. 400 but according to Kurt and Barbara Aland the Greek base of its text is thought by some to be traceable to the 2nd century (*The Text of the New Testament* (Grand Rapids: Eerdmans, 1989) 187). In Codex Bobiensis the words in Mark 16.8, 'and they said nothing to anyone', are absent. J. Keith Elliot suggested that another Old Latin MS, Codex Vercellensis (a), from the 4th century might also have originally contained only the short ending ('The Text and Language of the Endings to Mark's gospel', *TS* 27 (1971) 256).

[8] The long ending appears in modern English versions as Mark 16.9-20. The great majority of MSS are in this group, which includes all the Byzantine MSS.

[9] In this group are two 8th century MSS (L and Ψ), two 7th century MSS (099 and 0112), a few Coptic and Ethiopic MSS, and 1$^{1602}$, which is a Coptic-Greek bilingual lectionary of the 8th century. Also the miniscule 579 (13th century) has both endings. Some MSS (including Ψ, 099 and k) have 'he appeared' after 'Jesus' in the short ending. Some Coptic MSS and L do not have 'Amen' at the end of the short ending.

[10] For example, Maurice A. Robinson, 'The Long Ending of Mark as Canonical Verity', *Perspectives,* 40-79 ; Nicholas P. Lunn, *The Original Ending of Mark: A New Case for the Authenticity of Mark 16:9-20* (Eugene: Pickwick, 2014).

[11] Irenaeus, c. 180, cites Mark 16.19 (*Adv. Haer.* 3.10.6). Justin Martyr, c. 160, probably cites Mark 16.20 (*Apol.* 1.45). Also Tatian, c. 170, probably knew the long ending.

by transcription'.[12] James A Kelhoffer argued that the longer ending was added in the 2nd century.[13] Nicholas Lunn points to sectarians who were opposed to physical resurrection and considers that 'their deliberate removal of the resurrection narratives from copies of Mark circulating in Egypt would seem to be the most probable cause of the textual problem'.[14] N. Clayton Croy considered that the beginning and end of the gospel were lost because of accidental mutilation.[15] J. Keith Elliott considered that Mark's original gospel was accidentally shortened within the first 50 years of its composition and the later additions to the end and the beginning could have been made in the 2nd century. He speculated that Mark's original composition included 'a genealogy or a birth narrative of Jesus and even of John'.[16] In a more recent article he is convinced by Kelhoffer's argument that the longer ending is a 2nd century apocryphal text, and states, '[W]e must make it clear that it was inappropriately cobbled on as a conclusion that can scarcely be said to develop or belong to vv. 1-8'.[17]

Although Mark might have originally written his gospel on a roll or scroll it would soon have been produced as a book (codex).

---

[12] B. M. Metzger, *A Textual Commentary on the Greek New Testament* (London: United Bible Societies, 1975) 126.
[13] J. A. Kelhoffer, *Miracle and Mission* (Tubingen: Mohr Siebeck, 2000).
[14] Lunn, *Original Ending*, 360.
[15] N. C. Croy, *The Mutilation of Mark's Gospel* (Nashville: Abington, 2003).
[16] J. K. Elliott, 'Mark 1.1-3 – A Later Addition to the Gospel?' *NTS* 46 (2000) 584-88.
[17] Elliott, 'The Last Twelve Verses of Mark: Original or Not?' *Perspectives*, 98.

Graham M. Stanton states that 'use of the codex in the middle of the 1st century is perfectly possible'.[18] L. D. Reynolds and N. G. Wilson state that parchment notebooks (*membranae*) were in use in the 1st century BCE,[19] but the notebooks would also have been of papyrus. Although no surviving manuscript of the New Testament is earlier than the 2nd century, they are almost all in codex form.[20] According to Harry Y. Gamble, 'Most early papyrus codices are constructed on the single quire method'.[21] An example he mentions is P75 from the 3rd century which had the gospels of John and Luke in a single quire of 144 pages. As Mark's gospel is the shortest gospel it could have been written on only one quire. Therefore, if the last page is missing, the first page would be missing too.

    C. F. D. Moule found it difficult to believe that something had not been lost from Mark's gospel. He wrote, 'It is tempting to postulate a mutilation of Mark at the beginning as well as at the end. If one removes "The beginning of the gospel of Jesus Christ

---

[18] G. M. Stanton, *Jesus and Gospel* (Cambridge, Cambridge UP, 2004) 190.
[19] L. D. Reynolds and N. G. Wilson, *Scribes and Scholars; A Guide to the Transmission of Greek and Latin Literature* (Oxford: Clarendon Press, 1991) 34.
[20] According to Larry W. Hurtado a few are in the form of an episthograph, i.e. written on the back of a role to re-use writing material (*The Earliest Christian Artifacts: Manuscripts and Christian Origins* (Grand Rapids: Eerdmans, 2006) 57)
[21] H. Y. Gamble, *Books and Readers in the Early Church* (New Haven: Yale UP, 1995) 66.

the Son of God" – which is the sort of heading that any scribe might supply, if presented with only a mutilated exemplar to copy – , then the Gospel starts with a relative adverb, καθώς, "just as", which is no less abrupt and improbable as a beginning than γάρ (xvi 8) is as an ending'.[22]

The beginning of Mark's gospel as it is preserved in the most ancient manuscripts has several problems associated with it, which indicates that it might not be the original beginning. These problems include the following:

1. The first sentence is 'The beginning of the gospel about Jesus Christ, the Son of God', and (as Moule explained) if the first page of the gospel was missing then a statement like this would be necessary at the top of the new first page. If the outer leaf of the codex had been deliberately removed for some reason, this sentence would mean '*This* is the beginning of the gospel, and not any other text.'

2. The word 'gospel' (Greek: εὐαγγέλιον) in Mark 1.1 appears to refer to a literary genre that probably did not exist at the time of Mark's writing, although his account is usually considered to be the earliest example of the genre. This suggests a later hand, but the word also occurs in association

---

[22] C.F.D. Moule, *The Birth of the New Testament* (London: Continuum, 1981) 131 n.1.

with the imperial cult. For example, the phrase 'the beginning of the good news (εὐαγγέλια)' appears in an inscription dated 9 BCE from Priene referring to the birthday of Augustus.[23] This shows that the phrase was already known in the Roman world. If Mark 1:1 is ignored, the good news is the coming of the Kingdom of God in 1:15. If Mark 1:1 is accepted, then there are two lots of good news to believe. It is more likely that there was only one good news and that in Mark's original beginning the word εὐαγγέλιον is absent. For Mark the gospel is the coming of the Kingdom of God.[24]

3. In Mark 1.1 the word 'Christ' as part of the name 'Jesus Christ' does not occur elsewhere in Mark's gospel. The word does occur but it is not used in this way. Because the name 'Jesus Christ' is common in later writings it suggests a later hand in this instance.

---

[23] R. P. Martin, 'Gospel', *The New International Standard Bible Encyclopedia* (ed. G.W. Bromley; Grand Rapids: Eerdmans, 1982), vol. 2, 529.

[24] It is worth noting that in some ancient manuscripts including Papyrus 45 (3rd century), Codex Bezae (5th century) and the earliest Latin versions Jesus says that whoever loses his life for the gospel, will save it. (Mark 8:35) He does not say "for me and the gospel" as in the other manuscripts. In Matthew 16:26 and Luke 9:24 Jesus says only "for me".

4. The title 'Son of God' is absent from Codex Sinaiticus and some other manuscripts[25] but it was probably originally in Mark 1.1, which was written after the removal of the outer leaf of the codex. If the leaf was removed because Mark had described Jesus's birth as natural, which the Gentile Christians in Rome could not accept, 'Son of God' in 1.1 indicates the purpose of their action.

5. In Greek literature the word καθώς (just as) is used to link two statements; for example, 'The boy speaks just as his father does.' If the first verse had been inserted as Moule suggested, then καθώς could not be the first word. But if Mark had written the first verse, καθώς would link 'The beginning' with the Old Testament verses that follow, and that would make perfect sense. Mark probably did write the verse but not in the form that it is found in the New Testament today. What he probably wrote was: 'The beginning was according to the scriptures.' The original beginning of his gospel, which contained introductory information about Jesus, preceded this verse. This is a key point which will become clearer later in the book when the original beginning is reconstructed.

6. Mark 1.2 is a mistake. The prophet Isaiah did not write the prophecy in this verse. It was written by Malachi, and is

---

[25] Θ, 28 (corrected), some early versions and Church Fathers including Origen.

Malachi 3.1. It is unlikely that a writer would begin an account with such a blatant error. Naming only one author in a composite quotation might have been a Jewish practice but Matthew and Luke separate the quotations in their gospels (Mt 3:3 and 11:10, Lk 3:4 and 7:27) and Mark does not seem to be particularly Jewish. Therefore Malachi 3:1 was probably separate in Mark's original beginning. When the first page was removed the Malachi quotation was at the end of the page, but καθώς (just as) was on the next page. So the Malachi quotation was added as a gloss to the new first page when the new heading was written. Copyists of this mutilated and roughly corrected gospel began to realise that this was an unacceptable error and a number of ancient manuscripts such as Codex Alexandrinus, as well as all the Byzantine manuscripts, have 'in the prophets' instead of 'in the prophet Isaiah'. Various other explanations have been proposed by modern scholars for the insertion of Malachi 3.1 at the beginning of Mark's gospel. For example, William Lane states that 'it is commonly regarded as a very ancient gloss, interpolated into the text at so early a stage that it has left its mark on the entire manuscript tradition'.[26]

---

[26] W. L. Lane, *The Gospel of Mark* (Grand Rapids: Eerdmans, 1974) 46.

7. Who is this 'Jesus' who is suddenly introduced in Mark 1.9? Such an abrupt introduction might have been because Mark assumed that his readers knew who Jesus was, but 'Jesus' was a common Jewish name at the time. Although the later gospels of Matthew and Luke, which were largely copied from Mark, have long passages (often conflicting) about the parentage and birth of Jesus, there is nothing of that in Mark. Where someone was born and who his parents were would have been of considerable interest to ancient readers. Mary, the mother of Jesus, is mentioned by name only once in Mark's gospel (Mark 6.3) and Joseph is not mentioned at all.[27] It is the thesis of this paper that Mark had written about the parentage and birth of Jesus but this information was on the first page of his gospel, and when the outer leaf of the codex was pulled off the first and last pages were removed. It is unlikely that the outer leaf just fell off accidentally or was lost through wear and tear, as some scholars have suggested.

---

[27] The father was an important part of a person's identity. For example, the leader of the Second Jewish Revolt was Simon bar Kosiba. In Aramaic, 'bar' means 'son of', and therefore he was Simon son of Kosiba. Mark's gospel was written for Gentiles in Rome who would not have known that David had been the king of Israel about a thousand years before the time of Jesus, and when Bartimaeus calls Jesus son of David in Mark 10:47 they would have assumed that David was Jesus's biological father, unless, of course, Joseph had been mentioned in the beginning of the gospel.

The first and last pages of Mark's gospel could well have been deliberately removed, but how could this have been done when the last page was about the resurrection of Jesus Christ, which is vital to the Christian proclamation?

If the shorter ending was on the last page of the codex the person who pulled off the whole outer leaf would have been emboldened because there was little on the last page that could not be inferred from the preceding text. The Resurrection had occurred, although logically no one would ever know about it. The English translation of the Greek version of the shorter ending is: 'But to those around Peter they reported concisely all that they had been commanded. And afterward Jesus himself sent out through them, from east to west, the sacred and imperishable proclamation of eternal salvation.' The first sentence constitutes what would be a natural and logical addition to the previous sentence (Mark 16.8). In other words, the women were afraid to proclaim to everyone in general what the young man had told them, but to the special group close to Jesus, that is, those around Peter, they clearly reported everything. But the second sentence seems artificial: it is a brief statement added to the text to give a conclusion to the book, and its later and non-Markan origin is obvious.[28] The difference

---

[28] Eight words do not occur elsewhere in Mark's gospel. The word 'west' occurs nowhere else in the NT, and Henry Barclay Swete suggested that it pointed to Roman origin (*The Gospel according to St Mark* (London: Macmillan, 1913) cviii).

can be explained if the penultimate page of this particular codex of Mark's gospel did in fact end with ἐξήγγειλαν (they reported), and in the space below the last line the brief conclusion was written. There would have been plenty of space to write these concluding words because according to Hurtado the margins of Christian codices are generous and the bottom margin often larger than the top.[29]

Whatever was on the last page of Mark's gospel, and it could well have been much like the longer ending as found in most ancient manuscripts, the person who removed the whole outer leaf might not have considered it as significant as what was on the first page. His real purpose might have been to remove the first page, but why would he want to do this?

As previously suggested, he was probably a Roman Gentile, someone who was a fervent new Christian but who was imbued with Greco-Roman culture and religion. He could not accept what Mark wrote on the first page of his gospel. We do not, of course, know what was written there, but the likelihood is that it described Jesus's birth as natural. For Mark Jesus is declared to be the Son of God at his baptism (Mark 1.11). For Luke this occurs at his conception (Luke 1.35) and for John he is with God in the

---

[29] Hurtado, *Artifacts*, 169.

beginning. This chronology requires Jesus's birth to be natural for Mark.

In Mark's account of Jesus's baptism the Spirit descended into him, εἰς αὐτόν. According to J.D.G. Dunn, 'In the light of Markan usage elsewhere this almost certainly means "*into* him", with εἰς deliberately preferred to ἐπί'.[30] Matthew and Luke changed the preposition to ἐπι (upon), and John put ἔπεινεν (remained) before ἐπι to stress that the Spirit did not descend into Jesus. In commenting on Mark 1.10, R.T. France refers to the 'apparent absurdity of the imagery'[31] whereby Jesus sees a bird descending into himself, but Mark wrote that the Spirit was like a dove and the image of something fluttering is not absurd. Robert Gundry, in his commentary, accepts that εἰς means 'into', and points out that for Mark and his Gentile audience the dove is regarded in the Hellenistic world as a divine bird.[32] Also concerning Jesus's baptism it is worth noting that in Psalm 2.7 when God says, 'You are my son,' he adds, 'today I have begotten you.' (NRSV) For Mark, Jesus became the Son of God at his baptism and must have been born naturally.

---

[30] J.D.G. Dunn, *Baptism in the Holy Spirit* (London: SCM, 1970) 29, n. 22.
[31] R.T. France, *The Gospel of Mark: A Commentary on the Greek Text* (Grand Rapids: Eerdmans, 2002) 78.
[32] R. H. Gundry, *Mark: A Commentary on his Apology for the Cross* (Grand Rapids: Eerdmans, 1993) 49.

In the original beginning there might even have been some additional information, stated or implied, indicating that Jesus was illegitimate. In what remains of Mark's gospel there are clues that this might have been the case. For example, in Mark 6.3 the people of Nazareth refer to Jesus as 'the son of Mary'. According to John Shelby Spong, 'to designate Jesus "son of Mary", as this Markan text did, was quite unusual. Mark never mentioned Joseph. This could be an allusion to the possibility, or even the probability, that Jesus was known in Nazareth to be an illegitimate child'.[33] Although Mark never mentioned Joseph he is mentioned 15 times in the other gospels. In John's gospel (John 8.41b) and the Gospel of Thomas (Saying 105) there are more clues that Jesus might have been illegitimate. According to Jane Schaberg who was Professor of Religious Studies at Detroit University, 'The Jewish tradition of Jesus' illegitimacy is a strong one.'[34]

In the understanding of the person who removed the outer leaf of Mark's gospel, anybody of such significance as Jesus of Nazareth would have had a divine parent. Examples abounded in Greco-Roman religion where a god conceived a child with a mortal woman. The heroes conceived in this way were very popular. Heracles, the son of Zeus and a mortal woman, was

---

[33] J. S. Spong, *Born of a Woman: A Bishop Rethinks the Birth of Jesus* (New York: HarperCollins, 1992) 164.
[34] J. Schaberg, *The Illegitimacy of Jesus: A Feminist Theological Interpretation of the Infancy Narratives* (Sheffield: Sheffield Academic Press, 1995) 77.

particularly popular and his image appears on many ancient coins. Heracles (Hercules to the Romans) appears on all the silver coins issued in the name of Alexander the Great during his lifetime and for many years afterwards, and he appears on all the silver coins of Tyre from 126 BCE to 66 CE. Even the Roman emperors claimed to be the sons of divine fathers, and these claims appeared on their coins. The Jews had been expelled from Rome probably in 49 CE,[35] and for the Gentile Christians there Jesus could not be relegated to a lesser status. In later accounts of Jesus's birth, this 'defect' was corrected and Mary is impregnated by the Holy Spirit, not by a mortal man. It made Jesus literally and biologically the Son of God.

If the outer leaf of Mark's gospel was lost because of repeated use a lot of copies would have been made, but it seems that relatively few copies of Mark's gospel circulated in the first few centuries. Of all the papyrus fragments dated to before the 5$^{th}$ century there is only one of Mark. If the outer leaf was deliberately removed it must have been done at an early stage before many copies could be made. The person responsible probably did not act alone but belonged to a group of like-minded Gentile Christians. The matter must have been so important to them that any codices

---

[35] According to Acts 18.2 Claudius expelled the Jews from Rome. See also Suetonius, *Life of Claudius* 25.4. According to Orosius this occurred in 49 CE (*History* 7.6.15-16).

of Mark's gospel that they had access to were similarly dealt with. This group were so thorough in their work that no manuscript with Mark's original beginning exists.

If the last page was lost through wear and tear one would expect the copies to have various endings, and these variant readings to be reflected in the most ancient extant manuscripts, but they all have an ending precisely at 'for'. Where there is additional text it is often indicated by asterisks or other symbols. The autograph might well have disintegrated from overuse but that is irrelevant. Many documents from antiquity are damaged in some way, but Mark's autograph and the earliest copies did not survive and hence did not have to struggle against the ravages of time in order to exist for almost 2000 years. The argument for wear and tear is weakened by the fact that there are no textual problems with the beginnings and endings of the other gospels.

Because the primary purpose might have been to remove the first page of Mark's gospel, it is likely that the last page was kept by some in the group and later inserted as a loose leaf between the pages at the end of a codex or copied as an addendum into a subsequent codex. In this case the scribes would have been very suspicious of this extra text. They showed their hesitation to incorporate it into the gospel by putting asterisks, etc., around it. The scribes who copied Codex Vaticanus and Codex Sinaiticus omitted it altogether. In the Codex Vaticanus there is a large space at the end of Mark's gospel, possibly left by a scribe for the longer ending if required in the future. In some cases there might have been a delay (months or years) between removing the whole outer leaf and inserting or copying the loose page into the codex, and this would explain the existence of the shorter ending. The first sentence in the shorter ending was on the last lines of one of the codices that were mutilated, and in this codex the last word in the line was ἐξήγγειλαν (they reported), but when the loose page was inserted the brief conclusion (the second sentence in the shorter ending) had already been added. The second sentence in the shorter ending was probably written at the bottom of the page when the outer leaf of the codex was removed. If the last line of a mutilated codex ended with γάρ it would have been left as it was because the ending still made sense.

To restate the situation, if a loose leaf beginning with Ἀναστὰς (having risen) was inserted into a codex ending with γάρ (for), the shorter ending would be absent from the manuscript copied from this combination. But if it was inserted into a codex ending with 'they reported' (plus the brief conclusion) this combination would result in manuscripts containing the shorter and the longer endings. Understanding how these combinations occurred enables the textual problems at the end of Mark's gospel to be solved.

Following Swete[36] a number of scholars have remarked on the disconnection between Mark 16.8 and 16.9. Verse 9 begins with Ἀναστὰς (having risen) and has the pronoun 'he' not the name 'Jesus'. In some manuscripts (F, $f^{13}$ pm, aur, c, ff², and vg$^s$) the scribes have inserted ὁ Ἰησοῦς (Jesus) after Ἀναστὰς. On the disconnection Herman Hendrickx remarked, 'It is as if Jesus had been the subject of a preceding verse in which his resurrection was mentioned. This was most probably the case in the writing from which this text was taken'.[37] The most appropriate wording of the verse that preceded Ἀναστὰς would be: 'But they did not believe that Jesus had risen'. According to the thesis of the present article this verse would have been at the bottom of a page below the first sentence in the shorter ending. In the various manuscripts the line at the bottom of the page would have differed, as Hurtado explained, '[We] have no reason to assume that in copying a text a scribe tried to copy the same number of lines per page in all circumstances'.[38] Once this is understood the anomalies can be explained.

The verse that preceded Ἀναστὰς must have been: 'But they did not believe that Jesus had risen'. This sentence would be in keeping with the Markan theme of lack of understanding by the

---

[36] Swete, *Gospel*, 399.
[37] H. Hendrickx. *The Resurrection Narratives of the Synoptic Gospels* (London: Geoffrey Chapman, 1984) 105.
[38] Hurtado, *Artifacts*, 171.

disciples and it would have followed naturally after the first sentence in the shorter ending. A similar sentence, 'But they did not believe the women', occurs in Luke 24.11 when Mary Magdalene and the other women inform the apostles what they had been told. The combinations (shown in the diagram by arrows on page 45) were the most acceptable to these early Christians. Peter's followers in particular would not have approved of his disbelieving or of Jesus first appearing to Mary Magdalene whom Peter might have opposed. According to the Gospel of Mary, which Karen L. King dates to the first half of the $2^{nd}$ century,[39] Peter rejected Mary because he could not accept a woman in a teaching role.

Peter's followers might have inserted verse 34 into the last chapter of Luke's gospel so that the first appearance is to Peter, and the disciples' response to the report of the two men is the opposite of that in Mark 16.13b. In the last chapters of the gospels of Matthew and John the work of the pro-Peter group is also evident. They probably wrote the second sentence in the shorter ending of Mark's gospel because it gives the credit to 'those around Peter' in the first sentence and an ending at 16.8 reflects badly on Mary Magdalene. Members of Peter's faction in Rome

---

[39] K. L. King, *The Gospel of Mary of Magdala: Jesus and the First Woman Apostle* (Santa Rosa: Polebridge Press, 2003) 184.

would have been happy to remove the whole outer leaf of the codex. Moreover, this group would not have recommended that people read Mark's gospel because of its anti-Peter bias, and this might account for it being 'neglected' by the early church.

Instead of someone actually re-inserting a loose page into a mutilated codex, another explanation might be that at least one copy of the original manuscript escaped mutilation and this was the source of the ending that scribes later added to the 'received' texts that ended with 'for' and 'eternal salvation'. The copy of the original manuscript might have been a scroll with only the beginning missing, but this scenario is unlikely because one would expect the scribes to just copy the original ending, which did not contain the second part of the shorter ending and did contain the reconstructed sentence, 'but they did not believe that Jesus had risen', but there is no evidence that such a copy was ever made. It is more likely that instead of someone physically re-inserting a loose page into a codex, the scribes wrote at the end of the codices that they were producing, what was on the separate page. This separate page began with 'having risen' because the other pages beginning with 'but to those around Peter' and 'but they did not believe' had been destroyed by the pro-Peter group.

Another problem is the phrase, 'out of whom he had driven seven demons', in verse 9. Mary Magdalene had been named in verse 1 but it seems that she is being introduced in verse 9. It might simply mean that although she was a woman her testimony should have been accepted because she had been 'cleansed' by Jesus. In the Gospel of Mary (10.9) Levi rebukes Peter, saying, 'For if the Saviour made her worthy, who are you then for your part to reject her?'[40] It is unlikely that the phrase was a gloss from Luke 8.2 in view of Luke's general dependence on Mark. Although the phrase seems awkward at this point in Mark's account, if it was not in the original ending why would it have been inserted here? Luke probably copied the phrase from Mark and derived the gist of his Emmaus story (Luke 24.13-35) from verse 12. In verse 15 Jesus tells the disciples to preach the good news, which is what he proclaimed at the beginning in Mark 1.14, and in Mark 16.20 the disciples do go out and preach. Thus verse 20 provides a fitting conclusion to Mark's account of Jesus's mission, a more appropriate ending than 'they were afraid'. Just as Jesus's initial statement (Mark 1.15) is brief, so is his final statement (Mark 16.15).

The sentence, 'but they did not believe that Jesus had risen', which can be reconstructed between the first sentence in the shorter ending and 16.9, might be the key to understanding the original ending of Mark's gospel because together with 'they did not believe' in 16.11 and 16.13 there are three occasions in which

---

[40] Translation of Papyrus Berolinensis 8502 in King, *Gospel of Mary*, 17.

Peter and the other disciples deny Jesus. This could refer to 14:30-42: 'I tell you the truth . . . you will deny me three times . . . And all of them said the same . . . They went to a place called Gethsemane . . . He came a third time and said to them, "Are you still sleeping and resting? Enough!" . . . "Rise! Let us go!"' All of this is repeated in a post-resurrection setting after 16.8, but Jesus is more forceful. Instead of ἀπέχει (Enough!) the word in 16.14 is ὠνείδισεν (he rebuked). This is a strong word used previously by Mark in 15.32 where it means 'heaped insults on'. (NIV) Such language is reminiscent of 8.33 when Jesus rebuked Peter, calling him 'Satan'. Perhaps it was the word ὠνείδισεν that the Roman Christians found most objectionable about the ending of Mark's gospel because Jesus is scolding not only Peter but all the disciples, at least one of whom had already died as a martyr. Thus Mark 16.14 is good evidence of Markan authorship: it is unlikely that a scribe composing an ending for Mark's gospel would write in this way. With these insights it is apparent that the ending which Mark actually wrote was a 'wake-up call' to Jesus's followers in keeping with his last words to them before his crucifixion: "Rise! Let us go!"

The number three seems to be very significant in Mark's gospel. Jesus makes three predictions of his death in which he says "after three days". (Mark 8:31; 9:31; 10:33) Three disciples witness the Transfiguration and three women go to the tomb. In

Mark's original ending, three times the disciples do not believe that Jesus is alive. Although three was a sacred number symbolizing completeness (beginning, middle, end) there was probably a more specific reference, and it could well be the story of Elijah in 1 Kings 17:17-24. In that story there is an upper room and in that room a widow's son dies and comes to life after three actions by Elijah.

A persisting problem in Mark's gospel is that the young man's advice for the disciples to go into Galilee in 16.7 is not followed. But, as the missing sentence makes clear, the disciples did not believe what the women told them even though they concisely reported everything that the young man said. So, obviously, they did not go to Galilee. They stayed in Jerusalem and the conclusion of Mark's gospel takes place there. At the end of Luke's gospel (Luke 24.49) Jesus tells the disciples to stay in the city.

The disciples' lack of comprehension is highlighted in 16.14 by the word, ἀνακειμένοις (reclining at table), which had occurred previously at 14.18 when the disciples were at the Last Supper. Since they did not believe that Jesus was alive (16.11), they were eating food but it was not the spiritual food that Jesus had provided (14.22-24). They were ignoring Jesus's words at the Last Supper, which meant that he would live in them. Paul understood this when he said, 'Christ lives in me'. (Gal 2.20) In Luke's gospel the disciples on the way to Emmaus recognise Jesus only in the evening at supper when they receive the bread (Luke 24.30-31). In Matthew's gospel there is no post-crucifixion supper, and in John's gospel there is no Last Supper as in the synoptic gospels.

In the longer ending of Mark's gospel verses 16, 17 and 18 are probably a later insertion because the requirement of baptism would have come from the later Church, and deliberately handling snakes and drinking poison are mentioned nowhere else in the Bible. In any case they are not signs but examples of testing the Lord, which was forbidden (Deut 6.16). In commenting on Mark 16.17,18 Ched Myers wrote, 'Such "theological proof" is of course exactly what Mark's Jesus repudiates in his debate with the Pharisees in 8:11f.'[41] Moreover, in Mark 6.13 the disciples healed the sick by anointing them with oil, not by placing their hands on them. Perhaps it was when the scribes were copying verses 9 to 20 back into Mark's gospel that the list of signs was inserted because at that time the Church was consolidating and Christians were exorcising demons, speaking in tongues and healing the sick. In the excitement some might have expected to have other miraculous powers like those of the devotees of pagan healing cults that involved snakes. Verse 19 is authentic because Jesus sitting 'at the right hand of God' is the fulfilment of Psalm 110.1, which Jesus quotes in Mark 12.36. Also the phrase 'confirming the word' in

---

[41] C. Myers, *Binding the Strong Man: A Political Reading of Mark's Story of Jesus* (Maryknoll: Orbis Books, 1988) 403.

16.20 refers back to 'spoke the word' in 2.2. The mention of signs in verse 20 might have prompted the insertion of the list of signs in verse 17 and 18.

If one removes the second sentence from the shorter ending, adds the missing verse that naturally follows, and deletes verses 16, 17 and 18, it becomes apparent that the original ending is a brief but carefully crafted conclusion to the gospel. The final two verses contain the Ascension ('he was taken up into heaven') and the Coming of the Holy Spirit ('the Lord worked with them') in a compact form, which was later separated and expanded by Luke. The original ending, however, was consistent with the unflattering portrait of Peter and the disciples which is evident in the rest of the gospel, for example in Mark 8.33; 14.37; 14.66-72, and removing the last page would not have made much difference in that regard. The author of John 21 does make a significant difference by reinstating Peter three times. Moreover, he solves the problem of Galilee by having Jesus appear to the disciples 'by the Sea of Tiberias'. John 21 was obviously added to the end of John's gospel by a pro-Peter group (the 'we' in 21.24 who certified the gospel).

Probably the main reason for removing the outer leaf of Mark's codex was what was written in the beginning about Jesus's origins, that his birth was natural or that he was illegitimate. In any case the explanation for the abrupt ending of Mark's gospel presented in this article should give scholars reason for thinking that the beginning and ending were deliberately removed and that the gospel did not end with *they were afraid,* but continued with *but to those around Peter they reported concisely all that they had been commanded. But they did not believe that Jesus had risen. Having risen then early on the first day of the week he appeared first to Mary Magdalene, out of whom he had cast seven demons. She went and told those who had been with him and who were mourning and weeping. When they heard that Jesus was alive and that she had seen him, they did not believe it. Afterwards he appeared in a different form to two of them while they were walking in the country, and they went back and reported it to the rest, but they did not believe them. Later he appeared to the eleven as they were eating and he rebuked them for their lack of faith and hardness of heart because they did not believe those who had seen him after he had risen. He said to them, "Go into all the world and proclaim the good news to all creation." So then after the Lord Jesus had spoken to them he was taken up into heaven and sat at the right hand of God, but they went out and preached everywhere, while the Lord worked with them and confirmed the word by the signs that accompanied it.*

\* \* \* \* \*

The diagram on the following page shows how the various endings were formed.

|  |  |
|---|---|
| . . . . . . . . . . . . . . . .<br>. . . . . . . . . . . . . . γάρ. | NOT EXTANT<br>But to those around Peter they reported concisely all that they had been commanded.<br>*But they did not believe that Jesus had risen.*<br>'Αναστὰς δὲ . . . . . . . . . .<br>. . . . . . . . . . . . . . . . |

|  |  |
|---|---|
| . . . . . . . . . . . . . . . .<br>. . . . . . . . . . . . . . γάρ.<br>But to those around Peter they reported concisely all that they had been commanded.<br><br>And afterward Jesus himself sent out through them, from east to west, the sacred and imperishable proclamation of eternal salvation. | NOT EXTANT<br>*But they did not believe that Jesus had risen.*<br>'Αναστὰς δὲ . . . . . . . . . .<br>. . . . . . . . . . . . . . . . |

|  |  |
|---|---|
| NOT EXTANT<br>. . . . . . . . . . . . . . γάρ.<br>But to those around Peter they reported concisely all that they had been commanded.<br>*But they did not believe that Jesus had risen.* | 'Αναστὰς δὲ . . . . . . . . . .<br>. . . . . . . . . . . . . . . . |

*The words in italics are a reconstruction and are not in the extant manuscripts.*

# Bibliography

Aland, K. and Aland, B., *The Text of the New Testament* (Grand Rapids: Eerdmans, 1989).

Black, D.A., ed., *Perspectives on the Ending of Mark* (Nashville: Broadman & Holman, 2008).

Carson, D.A. and Moo, J.M., *An Introduction to the New Testament* (2$^{nd}$ ed.; Grand Rapids: Zondervan, 2005).

Cranfield, C.E.B., *The Gospel according to Saint Mark* (Cambridge: Cambridge U.P., 1979).

Crowe, B.D., *Was Jesus really born of a Virgin?* (Phillipsburg: R & R Publishing, 2013).

Croy, N.C., *The Mutilation of Mark's Gospel* (Nashville: Abington, 2003).

Danove, P.L., *The End of Mark's Story: A Methodological Study* (Leiden: Brill, 1993).

Dumdie, M.A., *Against Modern Heresies: The History of the Ancient Manuscripts of the Four Gospels and the Restoration of the Original Text* (2015).

Ehrman, B.D., *Jesus before the Gospels* (New York: HarperCollins, 2016).

Elliot, J.K., "The Text and Language of the Endings to Mark's Gospel," *TS* 27 (1971).

Elliot, J.K., "Mark 1.1-3 – A Later Addition to the Gospel?" in Black, D.A., ed., *Perspectives on the Ending of Mark* (Nashville: Broadman & Holman, 2008), 80-102.

Farmer, W.R., *The Last Twelve Verses of Mark* (Cambridge: Cambridge University Press: 1974).

France, R.T., *The Gospel of Mark: A Commentary on the Greek Text* (Grand Rapids: Eerdmans, 2002).

Gamble, H.Y., *Books and Readers in the Early Church* (New Haven: Yale UP, 1995).

Gundry, Robert H., *Mark: A Commentary on his Apology for the Cross* (Grand Rapids: Eerdmans, 1993).

Hendrickx, H., *The Resurrection Narratives of the Synoptic Gospels* (London: Geoffrey Chapman, 1984).

Hurtado, L.W., *The Earliest Christian Artifacts: Manuscripts and Christian Origins* (Grand Rapids: Eerdmans, 2006).

Institute for New Testament Textual Research, *Novum Testamentum Graece* (28th revised ed.; Münster, 2012).

Kelhoffer, J.A., *Miracle and Mission* (Tubingen: Mohr Siebeck, 2000).

King, K.L., *The Gospel of Mary of Magdala: Jesus and the First Woman Apostle* (Santa Rosa: Polebridge Press, 2003).

Kok. M.J., *The Gospel on the Margins: The Reception of Mark in the $2^{nd}$ century* (Minneapolis: Fortress Press, 2015), 42.

Lane, W.L., *The Gospel of Mark* (Grand Rapids: Eerdmans, 1974).

Lincoln, A.T., *Born of a Virgin? Reconceiving Jesus in the Bible, Tradition and Theology* (Grand Rapids: Eerdmans, 2013).

Lunn, N.P., *The Original Ending of Mark: A New Case for the Authenticity of Mark 16:9-20* (Eugene: Pickwick, 2014).

Martin, R.P., 'Gospel', *The New International Standard Bible Encyclopedia* (ed. G.W. Bromley; Grand Rapids: Eerdmans, 1982), vol. 2.

Metzger, B.M., *A Textual Commentary on the Greek New Testament* (London: United Bible Societies, 1975).

Morgan, R. "How did Mark End his Narrative?" *Exp Tim* 128 (2017) 417-426.

Moule, C.F.D., *The Birth of the New Testament* (3rd ed.; London: Continuum, 1981).

Perrin, N. and Duling, D.C. *The New Testament: An Introduction* (New York: Harcourt, Brace, Jovanovich, 1982).

Reynolds, L.D. and Wilson, N.G., *Scribes and Scholars: A Guide to the Transmission of Greek and Latin Literature* (3rd ed.; Oxford: Clarendon Press, 1991).

Robinson, M.A., "The Long Ending of Mark as Canonical Verity," in Black, D.A., ed., *Perspectives on the Ending of Mark* (Nashville: Broadman and Holman, 2008), 40-79.

Schaberg, J., *The Illegitimacy of Jesus: A Feminist Theological Interpretation of the Infancy Narratives* (Sheffield: Sheffield Academic Press, 1995).

Spong, J.S., *Born of a Woman: A Bishop Rethinks the Birth of Jesus* (New York: Harper Collins, 1992).

Stanton, G.M., *Jesus and Gospel* (Cambridge: Cambridge UP, 2004).

Swete, H.B., *The Gospel according to St Mark* (London: Macmillan, 1913).

Taylor, Vincent, *The Gospel according to St. Mark* (London: Macmillan, 1966).

Van der Horst, P.W., "Can a Book End with γαρ? A Note on Mark xvi:8," *JTS* 23 (1972) 121-24.

Wallace, D.B., "Mark 16:8 as the Conclusion to the Second Gospel," in Black, D.A., ed., *Perspectives on the Ending of Mark* (Nashville; Broadman & Holman, 2008) 1-39.

Wright, N.T., "The Resurrection of the Messiah," *TRev* 41.2 (1998) 107-56.

\* \* \* \* \*

# The Significance of the Missing Beginning and Disregarded Ending of Mark's Gospel

**Abstract**

The implications of my previous article, 'An Explanation for the Abrupt Ending of Mark's Gospel', are discussed. In the article it was argued that the outer leaf of the codex had been deliberately removed, thus removing the beginning and ending of the gospel. In this article the harmful effects of this action on Christianity are discussed. The status of women and the Christian understanding of human sexuality have been adversely affected and, disregarding what Mark originally wrote in the ending, has had a negative effect on Christianity.

**Introduction**

In the article, 'An Explanation for the Abrupt Ending of Mark's Gospel', it was argued that the beginning of the gospel was missing and that verses 16:9-20, which are considered by most modern scholars not to be the original ending, are (with modifications) the original ending. There are textual problems at the beginning of Mark's gospel and in some manuscripts it ends abruptly with γάρ (for), but others have in addition a short or long ending, or both. A new explanation was proposed: the whole outer leaf of the gospel was deliberately removed, thus removing the beginning and the end of the gospel. The reason for this action was that the disciples were portrayed as stubbornly not believing that Jesus had risen and that in the beginning Mark had described Jesus's birth as natural, which was unacceptable to the Gentile Christians in Rome. There might even have been an implication that Jesus's birth was illegitimate.

The first page of the gospel was destroyed but the last page of one of the codices was not, and at a later time it was copied back at the end of some manuscripts. Scribes were suspicious of this supplement, enclosing it with asterisks or not including it at all. The translators of modern versions have also been suspicious and usually include a note like the one in the New International Version: 'The most reliable early manuscripts and other ancient witnesses do not have Mark 16:9-20.' The New Jerusalem Bible (Reader's Edition) published in 1990 states that these verses 'are a summary of material gathered from other NT sources.' Scholarly commentators have followed suit and some even refuse to comment on verses after 16:8. The result has been that these very significant verses have been disregarded.

**The Missing Beginning**

Mark's gospel was the first to be written and the original beginning might have included some information about Jesus's origins: who his parents were and where he was born. If so, a natural birth would have been unacceptable to the Gentile Christians in Rome and probably a group of them removed the outer leaf of the codex. The story was then spread that just as Hercules and the other heroes of Greco-Roman mythology were the offspring of a divine being and a mortal woman, so was Jesus. This was written into the beginnings of the gospels of Matthew and Luke and became "gospel truth". It made Jesus literally and biologically the Son of God.

As Christianity spread in the Roman Empire converts from the Greco-Roman religion were enthusiastic about the new faith, and a natural birth would have been unacceptable to them because as John Dominic Crossan pointed out, 'A marvellous life and death demands and gets, in retrospect, a marvellous conception and birth.'[42]

Justin Martyr, writing in about 160 CE, believed in the virginal conception, i.e. that Jesus was conceived without sexual intercourse between a man and a woman; and according to Andrew Lincoln, "He undoubtedly held this view on the basis of

---

[42] John Dominic Crossan, *Jesus. A Revolutionary Biography* (San Francisco: HarperCollins, 1994), 6.

the accounts in what he calls 'the memoirs of the apostles' that were read in the assembly every Lord's day; 'having afterwards become man through the virgin, as we have learned from the memoirs' (*Dial*.105)."[43] The memoirs of the apostles would have been the gospels of Matthew and Luke. St Paul did not believe in the virginal conception because in Romans 8:14 he says that those who are led by the Spirit of God are sons of God. If ordinary human beings can share the title with Jesus there is no need for a virginal conception to attain it. According to Lincoln, "Paul has a high Christology, which includes the notion of the pre-existence of Christ, but a virginal conception plays no part in this and it is almost certain that he did not know of such a tradition. The earliest gospel, Mark, also shows no sign of knowledge of this tradition."[44]

In Mark's gospel an episode is recorded when Mary and Jesus's brothers "went to take charge of him, for they said, 'He is out of his mind.'" (Mark 3:21, NIV). If Mary had been told by an angel that she would miraculously conceive a son who would be called the Son of God (Luke 1:32) why would she behave in that way? And why did his relatives (presumably including Mary) not honour him when he was in Nazareth (Mark 6:4)? It is very significant that Matthew omitted the words 'among his relatives' when he copied Jesus's statement from Mark (Matthew 13:57b) and that

---

[43] Andrew T. Lincoln, *Born of a Virgin? Reconceiving Jesus in the Bible, tradition and Theology* (Grand Rapids: Eerdmans, 2013), 177.

[44] Lincoln, *Born*, 22.

Luke omitted 'among his relatives and in his own house' (Luke 4:24). It is also significant that Mary is not mentioned either directly or indirectly in Mark's gospel after 6:4.

In the 5$^{th}$ century the Virgin Mary was officially given the title 'Theotokos' (God Bearer) and widely considered to be the Queen of Heaven. Medieval portraits often show her wearing a crown. The result was that she was perceived to be the ideal woman and her sexless state was thought to be the highest level of womanhood. Any woman who indulged in sexual activity (even though married) was on a lower level, and for Christians human sexuality was confirmed as belonging to the realm of sin. Although the Gentile Christians in Rome who mutilated Mark's codex meant to raise the status of Jesus it also had the unfortunate effect of lowering the status of women.

In his book *Born of a Virgin* John Shelby Spong describes this development in the Church. In the final chapter he writes, "Only the church that manages to free itself from its sexist definition of women, anchored significantly in the Virgin Mary tradition, will survive. The virgin of a literal Bible, the virgin of the annunciation, Bethlehem, and the manger, corrupted by the years of an overlaid male theology, will have to go."[45] There is nothing new in these observations. The German post-Enlightenment

---

[45] John Shelby Spong, *Born of a Woman: A Bishop Rethinks the Virgin Birth and the Treatment of Women by a Male-Dominated Church* (New York: HarperCollins, 1992), 224.

theologian, Friedrich Schleiermacher, was well aware of the harmful effects of the doctrine of the Virginal Conception. He questioned how much of the current form of expression should be given up "because it is an addition not in itself essential, and harmful because the occasion of persistent misunderstandings."[46]

In the missing beginning of Mark's gospel there might have been some indication, stated or implied, that Jesus's birth was illegitimate. As explained in the previous article, there are several reasons for believing that this was the case. The immediate question is then "How could it have happened?" In her book *The illegitimacy of Jesus*, Jane Schaberg, who was Professor of Religious Studies at Detroit University, claimed that "The texts dealing with the origin of Jesus, Matt 1:1-25 and Luke 1:20-56 and 3:23-38 originally were about an illegitimate conception and not about a miraculous virginal conception."[47] She goes on to say that "Matthew was not thinking of a virgin conceiving miraculously. He was thinking rather of the law in Deut 22:23-27 concerning the rape of a betrothed virgin (*parthenos*), the law he presupposes in

---

[46] F. Schleiermacher, *The Christian Faith*, eds H. R. Macintosh and J. S. Stewart (London: T. & T. Clark, 1999), 390. This is a translation of the 2nd edition of 1830.
[47] Jane Schaberg, *The Illegitimacy of Jesus: A Feminist Theological Interpretation of the Infancy Narratives* (Sheffield: Sheffield Academic Press, 1995), 1.

his presentation of the dilemma of Joseph."[48] According to Professor Schaberg, Mary might have been raped.

As Christianity spread among the Gentiles of the Roman Empire the story of the virginal conception of Jesus was widely accepted. Differing accounts were not accepted, especially those originating in Jewish circles. In about 178 CE a pagan philosopher, Celsus, wrote *True Doctrine*, which was possibly based on early Jewish sources. In it he claimed that the mother of Jesus became pregnant by a soldier named "Panthera". "Panthera" was a fairly common name of Roman soldiers. According to Schaberg, the name "Jesus, son of Panthera" occurs in rabbinic literature before 200 CE and "the Jewish tradition of Jesus's illegitimacy is a strong one."[49] There is, therefore, the possibility that Jesus was conceived when Mary was raped by a Roman soldier,[50] but is there any historical circumstance in which this might have occurred?

When King Herod died in 4 BCE a period of anarchy followed. Sepphoris, a city just a few miles from Nazareth, was seized by rebels led by Judas, son of Ezekias. According to Josephus,[51] Varus, the Roman legate in Antioch, sent Roman legions into the area. They burned Sepphoris and sold its inhabitants into slavery.

---

[48] Schaberg, *Illegitimacy*, 71.
[49] Schaberg, *Illegitimacy*, 177.
[50] The name 'Panthera' is probably fictional because as John Dominic Crossan has pointed out (*Jesus,* 18) it is 'a mocking and reversed allusion to *parthenos,* the Greek word for the young woman from Isaiah 7:14.'
[51] Josephus, *Antiquities* 17.289.

Joseph, Jesus's legal father, lived in Nazareth and there is a tradition that Mary's parents lived in Sepphoris.[52] So the likelihood that a Jewish girl by the name of Mary was raped at that time by a Roman soldier is quite high.[53] But according to Matthew's gospel Herod was alive when Jesus was born because he ordered the killing of all the infants in Bethlehem. This story, however, could have been fabricated to indicate that Jesus's birth was like that of Moses, when Pharaoh ordered the death of the Hebrew boys in Egypt (Exodus 1:22), and to date it before the Sepphoris calamity. Therefore, if Herod died in the spring of 4 BCE Jesus would have been born early in 3 BCE.

Because Mary became pregnant before she was married she and Joseph might have left Nazareth to stay with relatives until the baby was born. Somewhere south of Jerusalem would have been far enough away, and Jesus could well have been born in Bethlehem. When Mary and Joseph left Nazareth the governor of

---

[52] Eric M. Meyer, ed., *Galilee through the Centuries: Confluence of Cultures* (Winona Lake: Eisenbrauns, 1999), 396-7.

[53] Soldiers have, of course, been raping the women of defeated enemies even in modern times, but accusing a Roman soldier of such an offence would have created difficulties for the early Christians because their survival depended on being pro-Roman. This is reflected in the gospels where Roman soldiers are portrayed favourably, for example in Matt 8:10. The crime needed to be covered up for various reasons and Sepphoris is mentioned nowhere in the New Testament.

Syria was Quinctilius not Quirinius as in Luke 2:2. Luke probably wrote 'Quinctilius' but a scribe copied it wrongly.[54]

If Matthew was aware of the circumstances of Jesus's conception, and especially if Mary had been raped by a Roman soldier, he would have created the story in Chapters 1 and 2 to counter the Jewish account and to complement developments in Rome where Mark's account of Jesus's birth had been suppressed by the Gentile Christians. If he was unaware of the circumstances he would have been faced with a historical vacuum which needed filling. According to R.T. France, "So obvious is Matthew's preoccupation with Scripture-fulfilment in these chapters that it is sometimes suggested that the 'facts' that he relates are themselves the product of his own imaginative study of the Scriptures . . . so that the virgin birth, the Magi, the flight to Egypt and the slaughter of the children are fictitious stories suggested to Matthew's lively imagination by the texts around which he relates them."[55] The ending of Matthew's gospel also suggests that the author was influenced by a group in Rome who followed Peter[56] because the disciples' response to what the women told them is not recorded.

---

[54] The scribe read ΛΙ as N. See my article, 'Publius Quinctilius Varus', in *The Australasian Coin & Banknote Magazine,* (July, 2019) 60-65.
[55] R.T. France, *The Gospel According to Matthew* (Leister: IVP, 1985), 70.
[56] That there was a pro-Peter group in Rome can be inferred from the situation in Corinth where a member of Peter's faction would say, "I follow Cephas." (1 Cor 1:12) In Rome Peter's faction might have become more powerful after the Jewish Revolt (66-70 CE).

The frightened women running to tell the disciples are stopped by Jesus who just repeats what the angel had already told them. (Matt 28:10) Then the gap between Matt 28:10 and 28:16 is filled by the pericope concerning the guards and the chief priests, and no shadow is cast on Peter's character. In Matt 16:19 Peter had been honoured by being given the keys of the kingdom of heaven. Although this gospel might have been originally written by a Jewish Christian in Syria, as most scholars agree,[57] it was subsequently redacted by the pro-Peter group in Rome. This is confirmed by the fact that the coin named in Matt 5:26 is a quadrans, which circulated only in Italy.

Matthew might have used a copy of Mark's gospel that was missing the first and last pages. This would explain the fanciful beginning and the jump from the frightened women to the disciples being in Galilee, which was according to what the angel had said in Mark 16:7. Luke, however, seems to know the original ending of Mark's gospel because the women are not believed, the two disciples are walking in the country, Jesus appears to the eleven in Jerusalem, and after addressing them he is taken up into heaven, but the first appearance of Jesus is to Peter not Mary Magdalene (Luke 24:34). Luke's account agrees to an extent with

---

[57] D.A. Carson and D.J. Moo, *An Introduction to the New Testament* (Grand Rapids: Zondervan, 2005), 151.

Mark's but as with Matthew's gospel it has been redacted by the pro-Peter group.

If Luke knew Mark's gospel it is likely that he also knew the original beginning and the genealogy that was probably in it. In Luke 3:23 there is the phrase, '[Jesus] being a son, so it was thought, of Joseph.' The Greek word for 'it was thought' is ἐνομίζετο and this word is used by Luke with the meaning that something untrue was believed. For example, in Acts 7:25, 'Moses thought that his own people would realise that God was using him to rescue them, but they did not.' If the phrase, 'it was thought', was originally in Mark's genealogy (before the idea of a virginal conception was promoted) then these words would have been enough to make the reader suspect that Jesus's birth was illegitimate. Luke would not have deleted the phrase because it accorded with the doctrine of the virginal conception, with which he apparently agreed. Luke could, of course, have added the phrase himself, but it illustrates how a few words can be very significant.

In Luke's gospel the section 1:5 - 2:52 deals with the miraculous births of John and Jesus. Luke inserted this section before the Markan material because he was probably a Greek and amenable to the idea of someone having a divine father, which was common in Greek mythology. Without the insertion then Luke 3:1, which establishes the time when John began his ministry, would have been at the beginning of Luke's gospel just after the introduction (Luke 1:1 - 1:4), and then Luke 3:2 - 4:13 would have followed and corresponded to Mark 1:1 - 1:13 (quotation from Isaiah; John the Baptist; Jesus's baptism and temptation). Luke inserted the genealogy (Luke 3:23-38) between the baptism and the temptation so that it comes just after the declaration that Jesus is God's Son, but it is late in the account to be providing all this genealogical information, the main purpose of which was to show that Jesus was descended from David (Matthew 1:1,6; cf. Mark 12:35). In Mark's gospel the genealogy would have been right at the beginning as it is in Matthew's gospel.

The descendants of King David are listed in 1 Chronicles 3 but the genealogies in Luke and Matthew are different. Mark's genealogy was probably like Matthew's which included the four disreputable women (Tamar, Rahab, Ruth and Bathsheba) and hints at something similar in Jesus's parentage. Luke must have objected to the mention of these women and its implication because he changed the genealogy to exclude them while retaining the key men, Zerubbabel and David. He followed what was probably Mark's order ('son of' not 'father of' as in Matthew) and extended the genealogy to Adam to include Gentiles.

A plausible reconstruction of the original beginning of Mark's gospel would be as follows: *Jesus of Nazareth was the son of Mary and, as it was thought, the son of Joseph to whom she was betrothed. Joseph was the son of [various names], the son of*

*David. When Jesus was about thirty years old he began his work. The beginning was according to the scriptures. It is written in Malachi, 'I will send my messenger ahead of you, who will prepare your way,' just as it is written in Isaiah the prophet, 'A voice of one calling in the desert, "Prepare the way for the Lord, make straight paths for him."' And so John appeared in the desert baptising...* An alternative beginning would be as follows: *Jesus of Nazareth was the son of Joseph and Mary. Joseph was the son of...*

An important consideration concerning the missing beginning is that a natural birth supports the conclusion that Mark's Christology was unorthodox i.e. the Holy Spirit entered into (εἰς) Jesus's body at his baptism. This would have contrasted with the orthodox view found in the other synoptic gospels and in John's gospel. In some manuscripts, including Codex Sinaiticus and the Byzantine manuscripts, in Mark 1:10 scribes have changed the preposition εἰς (into) to ἐπι (on or up to) in an effort to tone down the contrast. In fact, there are several places where scribes and the other gospel writers have changed the account to be more in keeping with orthodoxy, e.g. in Mark 10:18 Jesus asks, "Why do you call me good?" but in Matthew 19:17 he asks, "Why do you ask me about what is good?" With the formulation of the Rule of Faith in the 2$^{nd}$ century, orthodoxy became dominant and under such pressure Mark's original beginning could not survive. Similarly the

Ebionites, the Carpocratians and others who believed that Jesus was born naturally could not survive.

How do these insights influence Christian theology? For Mark, Jesus was born naturally and the Holy Spirit went into him at his baptism. Jesus was only a human being until his baptism when he became both human and divine. Actually there is no essential difference between Mark's understanding and the orthodox one that Jesus became human and divine at his conception. In the former the human side is fully human (i.e. the product of male and female chromosomes), but in the latter the human side is only from the female chromosomes. Also Mark's concept is simpler and more in keeping with Jewish thinking (e.g. 1 Samuel 16:13 when the Spirit came on David) but the outcome in both cases is that Jesus is human and divine. Mark emphasized the divinity of Jesus (e.g. 2:17, 2:28, 4:41, 14:62, 16:19) while believing that he was born naturally.

Jesus being baptized by John was embarrassing for the early Christians because it suggested that John was in some way superior to Jesus. Therefore we can be sure that it really happened. The purpose of the baptism was to prepare Jesus, the mature human being, to receive God's Spirit, to become his Son and be absorbed into the Trinity. As God is beyond time and space, the baptism was of eternal significance.

**The Disregarded Ending**

Concerning the ending of Mark's gospel and the way it was removed and re-inserted, it seems that two factions were involved. There was a pro-Peter group who removed the ending so that although the Resurrection had been announced the first appearance of the resurrected Christ was not to Mary Magdalene. Also the abrupt ending put the women in a bad light, Peter's three post-crucifixion denials were not recorded and Christ's scolding the disciples was expunged. In some of the codices a pro-Magdalene group was able to reinsert the last page which was critical of the male disciples. Actually, the whole of the gospel is so critical of the disciples that one suspects that the author belonged to this group that opposed Peter who had rejected Mary Magdalene.[58] The precise naming of the women in 15:40, 15:47 and 16:1 and the acknowledgment of their previous support and presence at the crucifixion in 15:41 suggest that women were influential in its authorship. Jewish women would have understood that Jesus's birth was natural and not the result of a divine being impregnating a mortal woman. Mary Magdalene, Joanna the wife of Herod's steward (Luke 8:3), or some of the other women mentioned might have been in Rome at some time and been the source of much of the information in Mark's gospel. Actually they might have

---

[58] Karen L. King, *The Gospel of Mary of Magdala: Jesus and the First Woman Apostle* (Santa Rosa: Polebridge Press, 2003), 17.

produced the gospel, which, of course, needed a man's name as its author to make it more acceptable in a male-dominated society. Crossan suggests that 'the unnamed woman in Mark 14:3-9 is "Mark" herself obliquely and indirectly signing her narrative.'[59] In 14:9 Jesus says that wherever the gospel is preached in the whole world she will be remembered, and in 16:15 he tells the disciples to go into all the world to preach the gospel to all creation.

Whoever the author was, he or she wanted the truth to be told even if some of it was confronting such as the mother of Jesus thinking he was mad and the men who were crucified with him heaping insults on him. Although the author was restricted by having to be pro-Roman and of course by having a pre-scientific world-view, modern readers can be assured that in essence it really is the good news of the coming of the Kingdom of God. Christians today can 'go into all the world and proclaim the good news to all creation' with their faith strengthened.

A possible scenario for the writing of Mark's gospel is as follows. When Peter escapes from prison during the reign of Agrippa I (37-44 CE) he goes to Rome accompanied by Mark.[60] When Peter preaches in the synagogues he is self-deprecating and admits that Jesus's disciples had not understood him. Many Gentiles are converted, but he causes so much division among the

---

[59] Crossan, *Jesus*, 192.
[60] J. W. Wenham, 'Did Peter go to Rome in A.D. 42?' *TynB* 23 (1972): 97-102.

Jews that Claudius expels the Jews from Rome in 49 CE. Peter attends the Jerusalem Council in 49 CE and does not return to Rome. Mark is associated with Paul for a time but falls out with him[61] and returns to Rome via Cyprus. He is influenced by Jewish Christian women when he writes his gospel for the Roman Gentiles. He then moves to Egypt sometime before Paul writes his letter to the Romans in about 57 CE.[62] After the fire of Rome in 64 CE Peter might have returned to be with the persecuted Christians.[63] After the Jewish war (66-70 CE) the influence of the Gentile Christians in Rome extends throughout the empire and any codices of Mark's gospel are mutilated by the pro-Peter group, but the pro-Magdalene group are able to re-insert the last page in at

---

[61] The falling-out was probably because Mark had been influenced by Peter and found it difficult to accommodate Paul's passionately-held views. Luke does not give an explanation for the falling out because his purpose is to describe a unified movement from Jerusalem to Rome, which accounts for his not mentioning Peter and Mark having been in Rome and for the enigmatic "he went to another place" in Acts 12:17. Also by discrediting Mark in Acts 15:38-40 he indicates the superiority of his own gospel.

[62] According to Eusebius, *Hist. Eccl.* 2.24.1, Mark was the administrator of the church at Alexandria until 61 CE. He might have been driven out of Rome by those who objected to his critical account of Peter, and Paul's reference to "those who cause divisions" (Rom 16:17) might have been directed at them.

[63] Peter probably did not return to Rome. The tradition of his martyrdom there would have developed from his being there in 42-49 CE. In *1 Peter* Mark and Peter are together in Rome (Babylon) at an apparently late stage but *1 Peter* was probably a pseudonymous document produced in Rome in the last quarter of the 1st century. The tradition of Peter having been martyred in Rome would, of course, give authority to the pro-Peter group there.

least one of the codices. The powerful pro-Peter group[64] promotes Matthew's gospel while tolerating Mark's gospel without its beginning and ending. Peter becomes 'the emerging figurehead of Roman Christians'.[65]

It is apparent that various factors were involved in the production of Mark's gospel and the other canonical gospels, and there is no doubt that the original texts were edited. Once this is recognised, rational examination of the gospels leads to a deeper understanding of the Christian movement and of Jesus himself. Because as Hans Küng stated, "No contradiction can be permitted between the Jesus of history and the Christ of faith,"[66] the historical Jesus should be able to influence the Christ of faith, even to the extent of deleting the word 'virgin' from the Creed.

Concerning the circumstances of Jesus's birth, Bishop Spong wrote, "They were circumstances over which he had no control, but circumstances which must obviously have shaped his life and

---

[64] The group would have acted as the Christian headquarters for the empire, like a protopapacy, editing the gospels so that Peter's primacy was affirmed. This group might have originally been the knights of Caesar mentioned in the fragment of Clement of Alexandria quoted by J. B. Orchard and H. Riley in *The Order of the Synoptics: Why Three Synoptic gospels?* (Macon: Mercer University Press, 1987), 131. According to Clement, Peter preached to the knights in Rome and it was they who asked Mark for a written record. They would have been very powerful people in Rome accustomed to the idea of divine sonship.

[65] M. J. Kok, *The Gospel on the Margins: The Reception of Mark in the 2$^{nd}$ century* (Minneapolis: Fortress Press, 2015), 142.

[66] L. Swidler, *Consensus in theology? A Dialogue with Hans Küng and Edward Schillebeeckx* (Philadelphia: Westminster, 1980) 7.

his sense of his own identity."[67] Jesus himself, when explaining that no one was to blame for a man being born blind said, "This happened so that the work of God might be displayed in his life." (John 9:3) Instead of insisting on the virginal conception of Jesus, which is really an unnecessary burden on faith,[68] modern Christians should agree with Saint Paul that, although distressing in many ways, the circumstances surrounding Jesus's life were all part of God's plan: "God chose what is low and despised in the world, things that are not, to reduce to nothing things that are." (1 Cor 1:28) In choosing what is low and despised in the world God might have added an illegitimate birth to being crucified as a criminal. To make matters worse He or She might have added being of mixed race or even being gay. An individual with such "qualifications" would indeed be able to empathise with others who might be suffering in similar circumstances. In other words, the Incarnation was not a superficial experience but plumbed the depths of the human condition.

God's plan is evident in the original ending of Mark's gospel, and the key word in understanding the process is ἀνακειμένοις

---

[67] Spong, *Born*, 171.
[68] Jesus can still be called "Son of God" even if he was conceived biologically in the normal way by the union of chromosomes. Otherwise the situation becomes ridiculous with divine amino acids, etc. According to Robert W. Funk, "The virgin birth of Jesus is an insult to modern intelligence and should be abandoned." ("The Coming Radical Reformation" in *The Fourth R*, July/August, 1998, p.2.)

(reclining) in 16:14. It has been translated to mean "as they were eating" (NIV) and it had occurred previously in 14:18 when the disciples were at the Last Supper. The importance of this word cannot be overestimated. Since the disciples did not believe that Jesus was alive (16:11) they were eating food but it was not the spiritual food that Jesus had provided for them (14:22-24). They were ignoring Jesus's words at the Last Supper, which meant that he would live in them. Paul grasped this central idea when he said in his letter to the Galatians, "Christ lives in me." (Gal 2:20) In Luke's gospel the disciples on the way to Emmaus recognise Jesus only in the evening when they receive the bread (Luke 24:30-31).

Jesus giving bread and wine and saying that they were his body and blood in a formal way (Mark 14:22-24) might not have actually occurred. He had been with his disciples in the fellowship meals they had shared together and they could have sensed that he was with them in this post-crucifixion meal. The formal institution of the Lord's Supper might have come later. However, in about 53 AD Paul wrote a letter in which he described the Lord's Supper (1 Cor. 11:23-25), which shows that it was already established in the mainstream Church by this time, and at about the same time Mark wrote his gospel. Jesus was expecting to die and probably said and did essentially what Mark recorded. The request (to eat his flesh and drink his blood) is so shocking that only Jesus could have made it.

Atheists could interpret Mark's original ending to mean that the Resurrection was just a psychological phenomenon that occurred in the minds of Jesus's disciples. It was a "light-bulb moment" that occurred when these distraught men were eating bread and drinking wine together and felt that Jesus was still with them. Atheists could also interpret the witness of Mary Magdalene in 16:9 as a psychological phenomenon because the appearance of a recently deceased loved one in a vision occurs occasionally to grief-stricken women. However, these atheists would be wrong in denying the activity of God because although the Resurrection certainly does occur in the mind of Christians, it is part of God's plan. In other words, God (or Creator, Mind, Being) arranged it.[69] He (or She or It) did it.[70]

It is important to understand that the basic premise of Christianity is that God is in Jesus Christ. The triune God was in the human Jesus. Although Mark described the Holy Spirit entering Jesus at his baptism the actual way that he became both human and divine would be beyond human comprehension. After his crucifixion he came alive through the sacrament of the Lord's Supper, and the Holy Spirit became active in the mind of his

---

[69] The empty tomb was also part of God's plan. Rather than the women going to the wrong tomb, it is more likely that the Jewish authorities ordered Jesus's body to be secretly removed to prevent the site becoming a rallying point for his followers. The young man in the tomb directed Jesus's followers to return to Galilee.

[70] Cf. Psalm 22:31, posterity will say that he has done it. (NRSV)

disciples. Just as evolution was guided in ways beyond the comprehension of human beings,[71] so were the Incarnation and Resurrection brought about.

In the original ending of Mark's gospel there are other words which confirm that God is acting according to his plan. In Jesus's final statement in 16:15 he commands the disciples to proclaim the good news (the coming of the Kingdom of God) to all creation. The message, therefore, must involve the whole universe, and in the final verse there are the words "the Lord worked with them". The significance of all this is that God is working with his people to change creation according to his plan.

With the Resurrection of Jesus Christ, God enters the human mind.[72] God and human beings become co-creators, extending God's work into the future and transforming the raw materials of the universe in ways unimaginable now but always guided by God and his plan.[73] The God-given tools that human beings might employ for this great task include quantum mechanics where the

---

[71] In his book, *Where the Conflict really lies* (Oxford: Oxford University Press, 2011), 39, the philosopher Alvin Plantinga wrote, "It is perfectly possible that the process of natural selection has been guided and superintended by God, and that it could not have produced our living world without that guidance."

[72] Spong says, "I find it both naïve and amazing that religious people today are unable to admit the reality of spiritual truth and psychic breakthrough to a new consciousness unless they can convince themselves that the biblical resurrection details were physical realities that occurred in an objective history that was bounded by time and space." *Eternal Life: A New Vision* (New York: HarperCollins, 2009), 179.

[73] "We know that in all things God works for good for those who love him, who are called *according to his purpose*." (Romans 8:28)

limitations of ordinary physical processes are transcended and human beings can reach into the universe.[74] The response of humankind to all this is worship together with prayer and Holy Communion, always aware of the prompting of God from the inside and the outside, the subjective and the objective, which constitute the experience of being alive.[75] God is spirit (John 4:24) and human beings must look for it within and beyond themselves, beyond the purely material. What is vital is that the connection with God be maintained because God is love (1 John 4:8) and with love comes goodness and truth. The aim is to realise the Kingdom of God.[76]

Although the pro-Peter group won the battle against the pro-Magdalene group and women were denied authority in the Church, it was not a total defeat because somehow the last page of Mark's gospel was preserved. It recorded that the first appearance of the risen Lord was to Mary Magdalene and that the eleven men were scolded by the Lord. Now that the page has been shown to be

---

[74] According to the eminent physicist, Neil Turok, *The Universe Within: From Quantum to Cosmos* (Sydney: Allen & Unwin, 2013), 91, "Our quantum future is awesome, and we are fortunate to be living at its inception."

[75] The theologian Paul Tournier describes the holy life as an adventure because "it is always on the alert, listening to God, to his voice and to his angels. It is an absorbing puzzle, an exciting search for signs of God." (Quoted in *The One Year Book of Encouragement* in the reading for 13th November, compiled by Harold Myra and published by Tyndale House in 2010.)

[76] According to Johann Metz, the Christian faith is 'an initiative for the passionate innovating and changing of the world toward the Kingdom of God.' (*Theology and the World* [New York: Herder and Herder, 1969] 93)

authentic the battle can begin again between the pro-women forces and the entrenched male hierarchy of the Church. Hopefully women will win the battle this time and achieve equality with men. Actually it could be argued that because it was a woman who announced the Resurrection to men who had denied Christ, women should be superior to men in the Church. Perhaps if women were in control it would be more effective in realising the Kingdom of God.

It was a great mistake that the Gentile Christians made in Rome when they removed the outer leaf of Mark's codex. The lost beginning would have emphasised the profundity of the Incarnation and prevented the wrongs that were done to women and others in society over the centuries. The humanity of Jesus would have been given more recognition, with greater attention to his teaching. Christianity would have been more inclusive and less dependent on miracles for its propagation. The rejection of the original ending that occurred in modern times (when people could actually read and understand the New Testament) has tended to deny women their rightful place in the Church and it has obscured for Christians the full significance of the Resurrection, that the Holy Spirit is in them and they are co-creators with God. As we go forward into the future we must remember the model that Christ gave us: loving, caring, forgiving, healing. This is what God intends human beings to be as they work with Her to transform the universe.

\* \* \* \* \*

# A New Appraisal of Mark's Gospel

Having read Mark's gospel in a critical way I have come to the conclusion that it is essentially true. It could well be what Mark remembered of Peter's preaching in Rome. It is the story of an extraordinary man, and it was told honestly by the original author within the limits of his time and pre-scientific world-view. Although the original text was interfered with in many ways, it can be reconstructed fairly easily.

The most drastic interference was the removal of the beginning and the ending as explained in the previous chapters of this book. Mark 1:1, 'The beginning of the gospel about Jesus Christ, the Son of God', was inserted by whoever removed the beginning of the gospel to provide an initial statement and emphasize that Jesus was the Son of God, but it contradicted what Jesus said in Mark 1:15, that the gospel (good news) is about the Kingdom of God being near. As Christianity spread and grew among the Gentiles in the Roman Empire the focus moved away from Jesus's message onto Jesus himself as a sort of semi-divine figure like Hercules and the other heroes of Greco-Roman religion. But Jesus was very different from them because he taught about the Kingdom of God.

What is the Kingdom of God? The answer is in Mark 12:29-34. When Jesus says to love God and neighbour, and a scribe agrees with him, Jesus goes on to say that the scribe is not far from the Kingdom of God: he is almost there. So the Kingdom of God is an ethical matter. It is about how we conduct our lives motivated by love.

When Jesus speaks about love (Greek: αγαπη agape) he means a self-giving concern for others, and this is what Jesus represents. He gives himself by healing and forgiving people and accepting everyone. But more than this: he gives himself to bring in the Kingdom of God. When he makes his triumphant entry into Jerusalem and disrupts the business in the Temple, he is provoking the authorities to kill him, but before they do he has a final fellowship meal with his followers. Jesus is the Love at the heart of it all.

Another significant interference in Mark's gospel is in Mark 14:27-31 where Jesus tells the disciples that they will all fall away and be scattered like sheep, but Peter says he will not fall away. To anyone reading this passage, verse 28 (But after I am raised up I will go ahead of you into Galilee) seems out of place. It supports the disciples and looks like an insertion by a pro-Peter group. That this is the case is confirmed by the absence of the verse in the Fayyum Fragment, which is from the 3rd century and is the only papyrus manuscript with the text of Mark's gospel after Chapter 12.

Mark 14:28 is significant because with 16:7 there are only two places where it is stated that Jesus will go ahead of the disciples into Galilee after he has been raised. Mark 16:7 has therefore been seen as confirming the prediction made in 14:28, but if Mark 14:28 is a later insertion, 16:7 must be critically considered in isolation.

Mark 16:7 is what the young man in the tomb said to the women. He told them that Jesus's body had been lifted and they should tell his followers to return to Galilee. If the Jewish authorities had removed Jesus's body to prevent the site becoming a rallying point for his followers that is what the man would have said. The tomb was below ground level because in John 20:5 the beloved disciple bends down to look into the tomb and in Luke 24:12 Peter bends down. The body would have been lifted up out of the tomb. The young man was presumably from Jerusalem and spoke in a different accent from the women who were from Galilee. When he said that Jesus was lifted up, the women misunderstood him and the rest is history.

That women were the source of much of the information in Mark's gospel is suggested by the statement in the Shorter Ending that the women reported concisely (συντομως) all that the man in the tomb had told them. How could anyone but the women know this? It is unlikely that they would have qualified their report to those around Peter by saying that they were speaking concisely. On such an important matter conciseness (and by implication, brevity) was the opposite of what was required. A complete detailed recounting should have occurred.

What is particularly significant about the word 'concisely' is that it implies that in some way the words spoken by the man were interpreted in order to exclude much of what he actually said. Such interpretation strengthens the suspicion that the women misunderstood what he was saying. The man meant that Jesus's body was literally lifted out of the tomb, but the women interpreted his words in the theological sense of him having been raised from the dead. It is significant that the man simply says that Jesus was lifted or raised (ἠγερθη), not that he has risen from the dead as in Matthew 28:7. Also he probably accused the disciples of stealing the body as in Matthew 28:13. That might be why the women fled from the tomb, said nothing to anyone and were afraid. Otherwise what were they afraid of?

Actually the very use of the word 'concisely' raises the question of just what did the women say. No doubt they believed they were telling the truth, but what really happened was that Jesus's body had been removed and the man told the women to tell his followers to return to Galilee where his body might have been taken. The frightened women kept the accusation of stealing to themselves until they reported to Peter. They would have spoken not only to Peter but to those around him, i.e. disciples, followers and anyone connected with them, presumably to counter the stealing accusation. All this supports the essential truthfulness of Mark's account.

The most important interference with Mark's gospel was the removal of the ending that Mark originally wrote. It corresponds (with some modifications) to 16:9-20 in most modern versions. In 16:15 Jesus tells the disciples to preach the good news, and this must surely be that the Kingdom of God has come. In Mark 16:19 Jesus is taken up to sit at the right hand of God, which is what he said to the high priest in 14:62. So the ending of Mark's gospel is about exaltation, and the model that Jesus provided (loving, forgiving, healing) is to be followed by those entering the Kingdom of God. It is the way they should conduct themselves. Then God will rule in their lives.

Jesus's exaltation in Mark 16:19 and his exaltation when he is lifted up on the cross refer back to the Transfiguration in 9:1-10. In that imaginary scenario Jesus is glorified on a mountain between Elijah and Moses, but on the cross he is glorified between two robbers (Mark 15:27). After both of these events his followers say nothing to anyone until after he has risen. (Mark 9:10 and 16:8).

The Transfiguration in turn refers back to Exodus 19 when Moses brings the people to meet with God. They stand at the foot of the mountain and God descends on it in fire. Then God speaks the Ten Commandments. In Exodus 19:16 God descends on the morning of the third day, and in Mark 16:9 it is early on the third day after the crucifixion that Jesus appears. Jesus has come down from the cross and the people meet with God in a spiritual way in Christ. The curtain of the Temple was torn in two (Mark 15:38) and God came forth from that holy place to be present with his people.

A careful reading of Mark's gospel shows that it is very profound. To understand it you should go as far as you can using the God-given gift of reason. Then you will find that your faith is strengthened. Read it with a free conscience; for St Paul reassures us, "Where the Spirit of the Lord is, there is freedom." (2 Cor 3:17b) Realizing that Mark's gospel was interfered with allows us to be realistic while still being aware that God was behind it all. We can be followers of Jesus without reading the Bible literally. Much of the New Testament is interpretation of what happened, and as Graham Long, the pastor of Sydney's Wayside Chapel, says, "Breaking free from any kind of fundamentalism brings marvellous liberation." Then the Holy Spirit can work in us to create the Kingdom that Jesus gave his life for.

# A Theological Reflection on the Ending of Mark's Gospel

All the synoptic gospels have the high priest asking Jesus if he is the Messiah (Mark 14:61, Matthew 26:63, Luke 22:67). In Mark Jesus says, "I am, and you will see the Son of Man sitting at the right hand of the Mighty One and coming on the clouds of heaven." In Matthew the "I am" is replaced by "Yes, it is as you say." In Luke Jesus says that if he told them they would not believe him, and he goes on to say, "But from now on the Son of Man will be seated at the right hand of the mighty God." Despite these differences, in all three gospels Jesus asserts that he will sit at the right hand of God, but only in the longer ending of Mark's gospel does this actually occur. In Mark 16:19 Jesus is taken up to heaven and sits at the right hand of God. This is what the reader expects: it is the logical conclusion to the story and it confirms that the longer ending is what Mark originally wrote. But why is the enthronement not in the endings of the gospels of Matthew and Luke?

It seems that Matthew did not know Mark's original ending because there is nothing in his gospel that relates to Mark's text after 16:8. Luke knows the original ending because the disciples do not believe the women (Luke 24:11), Jesus appears to two of his followers when they are walking in the country (Luke 24: 13-35) and the disciples stay in Jerusalem (Luke 24:49). But it is doubtful whether Luke has the Ascension at the end of his gospel because in 24:51 the words, "he was taken up into heaven," do not occur in some ancient manuscripts (Codex Sinaiticus, Codex Bezae and the Old Latin versions), but he certainly does not have, "he sat at the right hand of God." (Mark 16:19) Luke puts the Ascension in the beginning of Acts, which is the second part of the account that he wrote for Theophilus (Luke 1:3 and Acts 1:1).

In Acts 1:9, after Jesus spoke to the disciples "he was lifted up and a cloud took him out of their sight." Then two angels appear and the reader naturally expects them to say that Jesus now sits at the right hand of God, which is what he told the high priest (Luke 22:68), but instead they ask a stupid question, "Why are you standing looking into the sky?" What else would they be doing? Then the angels say that Jesus will come back in the same way as he went up. Why has Luke made such a significant change to Mark's account (Mark 16:19)?

To answer this question we need first to examine what Jesus said to the high priest in Mark 14:62. His first words were, "I am." This is what God said to Moses when he asked what was the name of God. God instructs Moses to tell the Israelites that 'I AM' has sent him to them (Exodus 3:14). This is God's name and although essentially a mystery it has the connotation of being alive, of being conscious and aware. It is an amazing statement for Jesus to make. It means that he thought he was God or in some way divine.

Then, in his answer to the high priest Jesus uses a mixed metaphor: he cannot be sitting and standing at the same time. Sitting at the right hand of God has the sense of permanence and stability, and this metaphor derives from Psalm 110:1, which Jesus quoted in Mark 12:36. Coming on clouds has the sense of movement and this metaphor derives from Daniel 7:13 – one like a son of man comes with the clouds of heaven. Obviously he would be standing not sitting.

In Luke's account of the Ascension Jesus goes up with a cloud and the angels say he will return with clouds (Acts 1:11). Jesus will be standing, as the disciples were at the time, not sitting on a throne. This is confirmed later in Luke's account because when Stephen is about to be killed he sees Jesus standing at the right hand of God (Acts 7:55). Why standing? He is standing because he is about to return.

Why has Luke changed Mark's description of Jesus sitting with God, to Jesus being about to return? To answer this question we have to understand the time and circumstances of Mark and Luke. Mark was writing in Rome before the Neronian persecution (64 CE) and the Jewish War (66-70 CE). Although there had been violence such as the killing of James in about 41 CE it paled in significance compared with the terrible events of the period 64-70 CE which climaxed in the destruction of the temple in Jerusalem. Mark's circumstances were fairly stable and this is reflected in the ending he wrote: Jesus is seated with God and the Kingdom of God has come. If Luke wrote during or after the Jewish War he would have been greatly affected by it, as was everyone involved in it. It was a horrible time and Luke with all the Christians would have turned to Jesus. The expectation that he would return was greatly heightened. In his First Letter to the Thessalonians Paul describes the event: the Lord will come down from heaven and the Christians who are still alive will be caught up in the clouds to meet with the Lord in the air (1 Thessalonians 4:16,17). Luke was one of Paul's companions and he too would have expected Jesus's imminent return, but to make his account more appealing to his readers he concludes it in 62 CE with Paul in Rome preaching the Kingdom of God, as Jesus commanded the disciples in Mark 16:15, and teaching about the Lord Jesus Christ (Acts 28:31).

The ending that Mark originally wrote is very significant for a theological understanding of his gospel. Jesus enthroned in heaven at God's right hand is what it is all about. Of course God does not sit on a throne in heaven as Zeus does on Mount Olympus, but the image symbolizes the Higher Power which is beyond the material world and of which Jesus Christ is the human face. Jesus is with God and of God.

It is amazing to think that Jesus did it all himself. He arranged the whole thing, i.e. the birth of Christianity was his doing. On three occasions (Mark 8:31; 9:31; 10:34) he said he would be killed and rise again: he knew it would happen because he was going to make it happen. With his staged entry into Jerusalem and his disrupting the business in the temple he provoked the authorities to kill him, and most importantly with his giving of himself at the Last Supper he carried it off. What an achievement!

It was not a group effort: his disciples did not understand him and fled when he was arrested. Even their following him was not their doing: Jesus commanded them to follow him (Mark 1:17). It was all part of his plan, and finally he sat down at the right hand of God. How bold! How confident! Whether God liked it or not Jesus installed himself, and we acknowledge him as Lord. But God did like it because, you see, God was Jesus.

God became a human being in order to become involved in the life of the world that he created and to guide it into the future. In this way human beings become co-creators with God in creating the Kingdom of God. Paul summed it up when he wrote that God was in Christ reconciling the world to himself (2 Cor 5:19a). God expressed his love by giving to human beings the model of Christ: caring, forgiving, healing, and by giving his Spirit. As Paul wrote in his Letter to the Ephesians, "Be imitators of God, therefore, as dearly loved children and live a life of love, just as Christ loved us and gave himself up for us. . ." (Eph 5:1)

God's Spirit is active in the world working through people. It is amazing how the Holy Spirit works behind the scenes prompting thoughts in people's minds. God gave his Spirit, but God is not in the business of protecting people from harm, in whatever form it might take. As Jesus said, if people want to be followers they must take up their cross and follow him. (Mark 8:34) We follow Jesus both objectively and subjectively. God is with us and in us as we create the Kingdom of God.

# The Denarius in Mark 12:15

**Abstract**

In the episode about paying taxes to the Romans, which is recorded in Mark 12:13-17 and parallels, Jesus asks to be shown a denarius. This was the standard silver coin that circulated in the Roman Empire at that time, and it is generally assumed that the denarius shown to Jesus was the common one issued by the emperor Tiberius. A case will be presented that the coin was not a denarius but a silver coin minted at Antioch and that once this change is made the whole incident can be seen in a different light. Why the episode was recorded in the way it was is explained, and a possible scenario for the writing of Mark's gospel is presented.

\* \* \* \* \*

In the episode about paying taxes to the Romans, which is recorded in Mark 12:13-17, Matthew 22:15-22, and Luke 20:20-26, Jesus asks to be shown a denarius. In numismatic circles this coin is known as the Tribute Penny because the subject of the episode is paying tax (tribute). It is called a penny because that was the word that the translators of the King James Version of the Bible used for the Greek word δηναριον (denarius). 'Denarius' was the Latin name of a silver coin that circulated in the Roman Empire. In the Greek manuscripts this Latin word was simply transliterated into Greek. When the King James Version was written the translators considered that the readers would not know what a denarius was and they used the word 'penny' because the readers would have been familiar with this coin, which was at that time a silver coin about the size of a denarius, and like the denarius it had an image of the ruler's head on it. The English penny had derived from the Roman denarius over the course of centuries, and a small 'd' is still written after the number to indicate 'pence'.

The briefest account of the incident in which Jesus was asked whether the Jews should pay taxes to the Romans is in Mark's gospel (Mark 12:13-17). The accounts in the gospels of Matthew and Luke are similar, but in Matthew's gospel, instead of "Bring me a denarius and let me look at it", there is "Show me the coin used for paying the tax." This is odd because it implies that each Jew was required to pay just one particular coin, but this would not have been the case. Although it is not known how the Roman tax system operated in the province of Syria, which included Judea, the Romans were a practical people and the Jews would have been taxed according to their ability to pay. There were wealthy Jews in Antioch and they would have paid much more tax than poor farmers who might have been required to give a proportion of their produce. The situation concerning the temple tax was quite different. This was the tax that every adult male was required to pay annually for the upkeep of the temple in Jerusalem. This was just one particular coin. According to Exodus 30:13, it was half a shekel. A shekel was equal to a tetradrachm (four drachms) and a drachm was the Greek equivalent of the Roman denarius. A half shekel was equal to a didrachm (two drachms). Both didrachms and tetradrachms were minted at Tyre, a Phoenician city on the coast. These Tyrian coins were the only ones acceptable to the temple authorities in Jerusalem, apparently because they were almost pure silver. Jesus and Peter paid their temple tax with a tetradrachm, called a stater in Matthew 17:27.

The didrachms and tetradrachms of Tyre had the head of a god, Heracles, on one side and an eagle, the symbol of Zeus, on the other (Figure 1), but these pagan images did not prevent the Jewish priests accepting the Tyrian coins as tax.[77]

---

[77] They were acceptable because the Jews did not *make* them or worship the images. The Second of the Ten Commandments (Exodus 20:4) was that they shall not *make* an idol in the form of anything in heaven or on earth and worship it.

Figure 1

In the incident recorded in Matthew's gospel when men came to Jesus and Peter to collect the temple tax, Jesus told Peter to find a stater in a fish's mouth and pay the tax for both of them with it, but Jesus might simply have meant that Peter should earn the money by fishing. According to Jewish law the making of images was forbidden, and that is why the bronze coins minted in Jewish areas in Jesus's time did not have human images on them although images of objects like palms and anchors were allowed. No silver coins were minted by the Jews until the Jewish Revolt in 66-70 CE. Presumably the Roman authorities accepted a variety of silver coins for their tax including the Tyrian ones and the coin in Mark 12:15 that had the head of the Roman emperor on it.

The accounts of the Roman tax episode in the gospels of Matthew, Mark and Luke differ in regard to the identity of the people who were questioning Jesus. In Matthew's gospel it is the Pharisees who sent their disciples with the Herodians. In Mark's gospel it is the chief priests, the scribes and the elders who sent the

Pharisees and Herodians. In Luke's gospel it is the scribes and the chief priests who sent spies. Although the combination of Pharisees and Herodians seems unlikely as they are generally considered to be opposed to each other, the gospels agree that the group of questioners consisted of Jews of various backgrounds.

Despite these differences the three gospel accounts are so similar in wording that biblical scholars have concluded that they are not independent accounts, and the consensus of opinion is that Mark wrote his gospel first and Matthew and Luke used Mark's gospel in writing their own. Therefore the person who was responsible for the name of the coin being 'denarius' was Mark, but who was Mark writing for?

There are several reasons for believing that Mark was writing in Rome for a Roman audience. This is either stated or implied in the early traditions about the gospel, which have Mark recording the preaching of Peter for those who had heard the apostle in Rome. For numismatic reasons it is clear that Mark was writing for Gentile Romans because of the way he uses the word 'quadrans' in the episode about the poor widow (Mark 12:41-44). 'Quadrans' is the name of a small bronze coin that circulated only in Italy. Also Mark translates Aramaic expressions and explains Jewish customs. Moreover there are many Latinisms in Mark's gospel. For example, in the episode about paying the Roman tax the word that Mark used for tax is κηνσος which is simply a transliteration of the

Latin word, 'census'. In Luke's version of the story he avoids this Latinism and uses the ordinary Greek word for tax, which is φορος (phoros). Similarly the word 'denarius' is simply a Latinism. Mark used this coin name because he knew that his readers would be familiar with it. He did exactly what the translators of the King James Version did when they changed 'denarius' to 'penny'. What this means is that the coin that was shown to Jesus might not have been a denarius at all.

Biblical scholars have simply accepted that the coin in Mark's account was a denarius, and the coin that is usually put forward as the Tribute Penny is the common denarius issued by Tiberius, who was the Roman emperor during Jesus's ministry. His predecessor, the emperor Augustus, also issued denarii with his face on the coins but it is much more likely that when Jesus made his famous statement, *Give to Caesar what is Caesar's and to God what is God's*, he was referring to the reigning emperor, not to one who had been dead for many years. The common denarius of Tiberius (Figure 2) has the head of Tiberius on the obverse.

Figure 2

The Latin inscription surrounding Tiberius' head is TI CAESAR DIVI AVG F AVGVSTVS. In the Latin inscriptions of this period 'U' was represented by 'V' and usually some words were abbreviated. The full wording would be TIBERIUS CAESAR DIVI AUGUSTI FILIUS AUGUSTUS, which translates as 'Tiberius Caesar, the son of the divine Augustus, the Augustus'. 'Augustus' was a title that was given to Tiberius' predecessor, Octavian, and used by subsequent emperors. Octavian had been deified after his death by Tiberius who was actually his stepson and son-in-law but had been adopted by him as his son to ensure his succession.

On the reverse of the coin there is a seated woman who holds a sceptre and a branch. The identity of this woman is unknown but it is generally assumed that she is Livia, the wife of Augustus and mother of Tiberius, although she may simply be the goddess Pax

(Peace). The reverse inscription is PONTIF MAXIM, which is short for PONTIFEX MAXIMUS, the greatest bridge-builder (to the gods). This was the title of the Roman high priest, and this office had been assumed by Octavian and all subsequent emperors up to the Christian emperor, Gratian (367-383 C.E.), who refused it.

If the common denarius of Tiberius is proposed as the Tribute Penny, then several problems arise. First, when Jesus asked the crowd whose portrait, εἰκων (image), was on the coin, the correct answer would have been, "Livia and Caesar." Second, the inscriptions are in abbreviated Latin, and very few people in Judea were able to read Latin. Therefore, the crowd would not have known what names or titles were on the coin. The common language of the people was Aramaic, although educated people knew Greek, which was the *lingua franca* of the Roman Empire. Greek inscriptions had frequently appeared on the coins that circulated in Judea from the time of the Jewish ruler, Alexander Jannaeus (103-76 B.C.E.), and Greek, not Latin, was the language written on the coins issued by the Roman governors of Judea. It is, therefore, quite likely that Jesus could read the Greek inscriptions on coins, but there is no reason to think that he could read Latin. Third, it is known that the denarii of Tiberius were minted at Lugdunum in Gaul, which was at the other end of the empire, and it seems very inefficient of the Roman authorities to be using these coins for the tax when facilities for minting silver coins existed at several cities in the Middle East. From 6 C.E. when Herod Archelaus was deposed by the Romans, Judea had been part of the Roman province of Syria, which at this time included Cilicia, and although the administrative centre of the province was Antioch there were other major cities that also had minting facilities, such as Tyre and Tarsus in Cilicia.

Most importantly, there is no evidence that denarii of Tiberius circulated in Judea at this time. None have ever been found in the hoards of coins discovered in Judea. According to Kenneth Lonnqvist, "The inspection of the Syro-Palestinian hoarding evidence from the $1^{st}$ century B.C. to $1^{st}$ century A.D. is also unequivocal in showing that no Roman denarii appear in any of the hoards prior to the 60s A.D."[78] He adds that even the recent excavations south of the Temple Mount and inside the Temple Mount in Jerusalem have not so far brought to light any new numismatic revelations. Also the site of Qumran, which is only about 15 miles to the east of Jerusalem, has been extensively excavated and although numerous coins have been found, dating from Seleucid to Roman times, not one was a denarius of Tiberius.

Thousands of coins have been found in Jerusalem, but only one was the common denarius of Tiberius. In regard to the few Roman

---

[78] Lonnqvist, K., *New Perspectives on the Roman Coinage on the Eastern Limes in the Late Republican and Roman Imperial Period.* Saarbrucken: VDM, 2009, 273.

denarii that were found from the Late Republican and Early Imperial Periods Lonnqvist explains, "None of the coins are, according to information I have obtained, archaeologically stratified or from clearly datable contexts, meaning that it is difficult to conclude how soon after minting they were circulated and eventually lost in Jerusalem."[79] Thus the single denarius of Tiberius that was found in Jerusalem could have been lost many years after the reign of Tiberius, and probably after the First Jewish War (66-70 C.E.) when conditions changed dramatically. The important point to be made is that it is only hoards that matter with regard to establishing the time when a particular coin circulated in an area. The conclusion that the denarius of Tiberius did not circulate in Jerusalem is supported by the results of a survey of coin finds in Jerusalem by Donald Ariel of the Israel Department of Antiquities who noted the complete absence of Roman coin hoards in Jerusalem before 70 C.E.[80] In 2013, in a personal communication, Danny Syon, Head of the Scientific Assessment Branch of the Israel Antiquities Authority, wrote, "There is just *one* (this is not a mistake) denarius of Tiberius in the entire Israel state collections, find spot unknown. While I do not claim that there were not some more of these (private collectors surely have a few), their number in this part of the world was very

---
[79] Lonnqvist, New Perspectives, 272.
[80] Ariel, D., "A Survey of Coin Finds in Jerusalem." *Liber Annuus* 32 (1982) 273-326.

low. Of course we have the 'Isfiyya hoard too. It would seem that Roman *denarii* and *aurei* did not arrive in the east before c. 70 CE in any appreciable numbers. In contrast, the Bar-Kokhba coinage – overstruck on *denarii* and drachms – shows that by 132 CE they were very much common. It is hard to claim that all denarii of the $1^{st}$ century disappeared, but those of the $2^{nd}$ and $3^{rd}$ centuries survived."

A hoard of coins, called the 'Isfiya hoard after the nearby village, was discovered in the Mt. Carmel area in northern Israel in 1960. It contained about 4500 ancient silver coins. Although its exact composition is unknown Cecilia Meir considers that it originally contained about 3500 tetradrachms of Tyre, 1000 didrachms of Tyre, and 160 early Imperial denarii struck at the mint of Lugdunum.[81] The last group contained denarii of Augustus and Tiberius. The Tyrian coins bore dates up to about 52/53 C.E. and the hoard was probably buried some years later. Obviously this hoard is very unusual and its significance is difficult to determine. Its location was closer to Tyre than to Jerusalem and it was certainly not representative of what a Jew in Jerusalem might have in his or her purse during the reign of Tiberius.

The finding that Augustan and Tiberian denarii did not circulate in the province of Syria during the lifetime of Jesus (*c*. 5 B.C.E. to

---

[81] Meir, C., "Tyrian Sheqels and half Shekels with Unpublished Dates from the 'Isfiya Hoard in the Kadman Numismatic Pavilion." *Israel Numismatic Research* 3 (2008) 117.

30 C.E.) suggests that the province was a closed currency area at the time. This means that coins minted outside the province were not allowed to circulate inside the province. Foreigners arriving at entry points such as Tyre, Seleucia (the port for Antioch) or Caesarea Maritima would have been required to change their money into the currency of the province. Presumably the foreign money was then melted down and minted into the local currency, or it would have been returned to Rome or to a city in the Roman Empire where the coins were in circulation. Egypt was such a closed currency area.[82] It had its own bronze and silver coinage which circulated only in that province.

It might be argued that the money changers who were installed in the precincts of the temple in Jerusalem would have been changing denarii into the local currency, and therefore when Jesus asked for a denarius one would have been readily available from the money changers or their customers. There are several weaknesses in this argument. First, it is very unlikely that Jesus would have called for an object bearing an image of the emperor, especially in the precincts of the temple, because such images were forbidden. The Jewish people must have understood the Law as not allowing any human images in Jerusalem because the Jewish historian, Flavius Josephus, recorded the reaction of the people

---

[82] Burnett, A., Amandry, M. and Ripolles, P., *Roman Provincial Coinage*. London / Paris: British Museum and Bibliothèque Nationale de France, 1992, 1.13.

when Pontius Pilate brought standards bearing the image of the emperor Tiberius into the city.[83] The Jews said they would rather die than their laws be transgressed. Second, he would have been a brave or foolish man to produce an object bearing the emperor's image under these circumstances, which could not have been more dangerous. He was standing in the court of the temple making a public gesture in the presence of Pharisees, who were very strict in their observance of the Law and were looking for any transgression. Third, it is inconceivable that Jesus would have had anything to do with the money changers or their activities. In his gospel Mark records that on one occasion Jesus overturned the tables of the money changers and the benches of those selling doves, and would not allow anyone to carry merchandise through the temple courts (Mark 11.16). Exactly what the money changers were doing is unknown. They might have been changing the local bronze coins into the Tyrian didrachms and tetradrachms required for the temple tax, or they might have been facilitating the financial transactions involved in the buying and selling of sacrificial animals. Also the people might have needed Tyrian silver coins to pay their taxes to the Romans.

According to the account in Mark's gospel the people who asked Jesus about paying taxes to the Romans were Pharisees and Herodians. The Herodians are first mentioned in Mark's gospel

---

[83] Josephus, Flavius, *Jewish Antiquities*, 5.55-59.

when Jesus was teaching in Galilee (Mark 3.6) and this led to the suggestion that the incident about paying taxes might have occurred in Galilee. But C. E. B. Cranfield in his commentary on Mark's gospel states, "The presence of partisans of Herod Antipas is no reason for thinking that this incident must have taken place in Galilee; for they would naturally be in Jerusalem for the feast."[84] The feast was the Passover, and Herod Antipas would have been in Jerusalem at that time (Luke 23:7). So there is no reason to doubt that the incident about paying taxes occurred in Jerusalem. For the Passover festival Jews regularly travelled to Jerusalem from all parts of the province and beyond. There would have been Jews from Antioch, the provincial capital, where there was a large Jewish community.

Few scholars have doubted that the Tribute Penny was a denarius for the simple reason that there seemed to be no alternative. The coin must have had the image of the Roman emperor on it, but the Tyrian silver coins that are known to have circulated in Jerusalem and the adjacent Jewish areas did not bear his image. Large numbers of silver coins were minted in Antioch and other cities in the north of the province, and they bore the emperor's image, but they did not circulate in the southern Jewish areas. No coins of Antioch have been found in hoards in these

---

[84] Cranfield, C.E.B., *The Gospel according to Saint Mark: An Introduction and Commentary.* Cambridge: Cambridge University, 1959, 369.

areas before Nero's reign (54-68 C.E.) when the Roman authorities decided to replace the Tyrian silver coinage with coins that were minted in Antioch. In summary, the northern part of the province had silver coins with the emperor's image on them while the southern part did not. This created a problem for scholars.

Two scholars who have recently considered it unlikely that the Tribute Penny was a denarius are Richard Abdy, who is Curator of Roman Coins in the British Museum, and Amelis Dowler, who is Curator of Greek Coins. In their 2013 book[85] they suggested that the coin was a Syrian tetradrachm with Zeus on the reverse. As will be explained in this paper it is much more likely that the coin was a Syrian tetradrachm with an image of the deified Augustus on the reverse.

The key to solving this problem is to be found in the *Gospel of Thomas*. Although a few fragments of this gospel in the original Greek were known to scholars, the whole gospel in Coptic was discovered in 1945 in Egypt. The first Greek edition was probably written in the early part of the 2nd century and it seems that the Christians who used it were influenced by Gnosticism, which stressed the importance of secret knowledge. In this gospel, which is a collection of sayings purported to be from Jesus rather than a narrative account like Mark's gospel, salvation depends on a true

---

[85] Abdy, R. and Dowler, A., *Coins and the Bible*. London: The British Museum and Spink, 2013, 50.

understanding of these sayings. Nevertheless, many biblical scholars consider that it does contain information that was not simply copied from the synoptic gospels but derives from the earliest strata of Christian history. In this regard Stephen Patterson writes, "Thomas' sayings often exhibit characteristics of a secondary nature, but with few exceptions these secondary features are unique to the Thomas version, and have affixed themselves to a form of the saying which is itself more primitive than the synoptic version."[86]

In the *Gospel of Thomas* there is a passage (logion 100) that deals with the incident about paying taxes to the Romans: *They showed Jesus a gold coin and said to him, "The Roman emperor's people demand taxes from us." He said to them, "Give the emperor what belongs to the emperor, give God what belongs to God, and give me what is mine."*[87] The Coptic word which has here been translated as 'a gold coin' could be translated simply as 'a coin'.[88] The word 'they', when it occurs in the *Gospel of*

---

[86] Patterson, S., in J. Kloppenborg et al., *Q Thomas Reader.* Sonoma: Polebridge Press, 1990, 87.
[87] This is the translation of the Coptic text that is known as the Scholars Version.
[88] In a personal communication, Einar Thomassen, who is Professor of Religion at the University of Bergen and one of the translators of the International Edition of The Nag Hammadi Scriptures wrote, "[T]he Coptic word that is used is noub, which literally means 'gold', and with the indefinite article 'a piece of gold'. Crum's Coptic Dictionary (221b), however, suggests that the word may also be used simply as a name for 'money' or 'coin' in general, and the examples he gives support this. Thus, 'gold' is used metonymically for

*Thomas*, refers to outside persons, while the disciples are referred to as 'the disciples'. The only phrase in the above translation that lacks a parallel in the synoptic gospels is 'give me what is mine.' This phrase was probably added when the Gnosticising tendency in Thomas Christianity became stronger, because it is difficult to imagine the historical Jesus saying this. But the important point to be made here is that showing the coin occurs before any question about paying taxes. Thus it was the coin that was the cause of the whole incident. It was not just an incidental prop that was used by Jesus. A group of Jews brought the coin to show it to him and ask him about it.

In Mark's version of the incident there may be remnants of the original account in which the coin precedes the question. The phrase 'You pay no attention to who they are' (NIV), which in Greek is οὐ βλεπεις εἰς προσωπον ανθρωπων and literally means 'You do not look at a face of men', could refer to Jesus's reluctance to look at the human image on a coin. In Luke's version the corresponding Greek text is οὐ λαμβανεις προσωπον, which is literally 'You do not receive a face'. These Greek phrases are generally considered by scholars to reflect Hebraic idiom. They may, however, be echoes of the original account in which Jesus did not want to receive the coin and look at the human face on it.

---

'money', and 'piece of gold' for 'coin'." In any case it is most unlikely that a gold coin would be produced in the context of Jesus with a group of Jews.

Concerning this phrase in the Greek text of Mark's gospel, Robert Gundry considers that it "produces a double reference to not gazing at sidelong facial images stamped on Roman coins but prohibited by the Mosaic law as well as to not showing favouritism."[89] If this is so, then there is a reference in Mark's account to a coin even before any utterance of Jesus.

Another remnant of the original account might be the long preliminary speech in Mark's version: "Teacher, we know you are a man of integrity. You aren't swayed by men, because you pay no attention to who they are; but you teach the way of God in accordance with the truth." In Mark's gospel this speech becomes a piece of flattery intended to induce Jesus to relax his guard and fall into a trap. It does, however, have a sincere ring to it, reflecting the belief that Jesus really was teaching the truth.[90] In this case it was intended to persuade Jesus to look at the coin that had been brought to him, even though he might be transgressing the Jewish law in doing so. Such remnants or echoes suggest that Mark had written notes in front of him when he wrote his version of the incident, and Mark could have made these notes when Peter was preaching in the synagogues in Rome.

---

[89] Gundry, R.H., *Mark: A Commentary on his Apology for the Cross*. Grand Rapids: Eerdmans, 1993, 693.
[90] In John 14:6 Jesus refers to himself as 'the Way', and this was the term used by the first Christians for their sect. (Acts 9:2, etc.)

But who brought the coin to Jesus and what coin was it? They were probably Jews who had come from Antioch for the Passover and they brought a coin that had recently been issued there. It had the head of Tiberius on the obverse, and on the reverse, the head of Octavian (Augustus) with the claim that he was God (or a god). The coin is number 4161 in the comprehensive catalogue, *Roman Provincial Coinage*.[91] Hereafter it will be referred to as RPC 4161. It was the only silver coin minted at Antioch by Tiberius during the lifetime of Jesus. Most interpreters place the composition of the *Gospel of Thomas* in Syria[92] and therefore Antioch could well have been where logion 100 originated. Some numismatists[93] consider that it is more likely that RPC 4161 was minted not in Antioch but in another city in the north of the province, but the exact site of the mint does not matter. The coin would have circulated in Antioch and other places where there were Jewish communities, and they would have been aghast at it. No coin issued by the Roman authorities in Syria had made that claim before. The coins of Antiochus IV (175-164 BCE), who was much

---

[91] Burnett, A., et al., *Roman Provincial Coinage, Volume I, Part I*. London and Paris: British Museum Press and Bibliothèque nationale de France, 1992, 614.

[92] Van Voorst, R.E., "The New Testament Apocrypha", in *Eerdmans Commentary on the Bible* edited by J.D.G. Dunn and J.W. Rogerson. Grand Rapids: Eerdmans, 2003, 1574.

[93] Butcher, K., *Coinage in Roman Syria*. London: Royal Numismatic Society, 2004, 61; McAlee, R., *The Coins of Roman Antioch*. Lancaster PA: Classical Numismatic Group, 2007, 122.

hated by the Jews, claimed that he was divine although a human being. The gods on the coins that Jews used in the province of Syria during Tiberius's reign, e.g. the tetradrachms of Tyre, had not been human and would have been perceived by them as part of other religions. RPC 4161 was different in that it made a claim that concerned all the subjects of the Roman emperor, who was a human being.

RPC 4161 is a silver tetradrachm containing a fairly high percentage of silver. On the obverse there is the laureate head of Tiberius with the surrounding Greek inscription, ΤΙΒΕΡΙΟΣ ΣΕΒΑΣΤΟΣ ΚΑΙΣΑΡ (Tiberius, Augustus, Caesar). On the reverse there is the head of Augustus wearing a radiate crown signifying that he has been deified. The surrounding Greek inscription is ΘΕΟΣ ΣΕΒΑΣΤΟΣ ΚΑΙΣΑΡ (God, Augustus, Caesar). The coin is rare today. There are only about a dozen known examples. There are two in the Collection of St John's Cathedral in Brisbane (Figure 3), one in the Royal Collection of Coins and Medals in the Danish National Museum in Copenhagen, one in the Museum of the American Numismatic Society in New York, and the rest are in private hands.

Figure 3

A possible explanation for the rarity of RPC 4161 today is that the Jews understood Jesus's statement to mean that they should protest to the Roman authorities in Antioch, and as a result the coin was withdrawn from circulation, no doubt with the enthusiastic assistance of the Jews. It might seem out of character for the Romans to have backed down in this way, but Tiberius was a pragmatic man, and he would not have wanted a Jewish rebellion on his hands, and refusing to pay taxes to the Romans was tantamount to rebellion. Nor would he have wanted to antagonise the wealthy Jews of Antioch whose problem was not that they paid tax but the coins used for paying the tax. Also, according to the 2$^{nd}$ century historian, Suetonius, Tiberius lacked any deep regard for the gods or other religions, and hated flattery.[94] He would not have enforced such a matter, which was of little importance to him but of great religious significance to the Jews.

---

[94] Suetonius, *The Twelve Caesars*. London: Penguin, 1957, 129 and 149.

Since the Reformation, Jesus's statement, *Give to Caesar what is Caesar's and to God what is God's*, has been interpreted as advocating the separation of Church and State, in which case the people should not object because God's domain is quite separate. Although Jesus's pronouncement is arresting and memorable, it is not at all clear what he means. If the Tribute Penny is the blasphemous coin, RPC 4161, then it seems likely that Jesus meant by the first part of his answer that the Jews should continue to pay taxes to the Romans, and by the second part that they should object that their religion was being disregarded in this way. Actually this interpretation could also be derived from the denarius of Tiberius because the inscription on the obverse claims that Tiberius is the son of a god, which would have made it objectionable to the Jews; but on the denarius it is written in abbreviated Latin and in any case the coin did not circulate in Judaea. The idea behind giving to Caesar what is his is that if something had a person's name on it, it still belonged to that person whatever someone else might have done to earn it.

The Tribute Penny could not have been one of the more common tetradrachms issued at Antioch during the reign of the emperor Augustus (27 B.C.E. - 14 C.E.) because on some of these coins there is the statement in Greek that the coin belonged to Caesar Augustus and the people of Antioch. In this case Jesus's pronouncement, *Give to Caesar what is Caesar's*, would be contradicting what was plainly inscribed on the coin. One would have to argue that Jesus knew in advance that the coin that would be brought to him was one without this inscription.

If it is accepted that the coin in the episode about paying tax was RPC 4161 and that it was shown to Jesus for his advice, then the whole incident can be seen in a different light, and certain inferences can be made. First, the Jews who were questioning Jesus were not trying to trap him with the intention of having him arrested and killed. Obviously at some later stage this might have been the intention of the leading Jews in Jerusalem because he was crucified by the Romans apparently at the instigation of the Jews, but early in his ministry Jesus would have been considered just another Jewish holy man.

Soon after the beginning of Mark's gospel it is stated that the Pharisees went out and began to plot with the Herodians how they might kill Jesus (Mark 3:6), but this reflects the situation at a much later date when there was much animosity between the Jews and Christians in Rome, where Mark was writing his gospel. As early as the reign of the emperor Claudius (41-54 C.E.) there were disturbances in Rome between the Jews and the Christians. These were serious because Suetonius records that because the Jews at Rome caused continuous disturbances at the instigation of

'Chrestus', Claudius ordered the Jews to leave Rome.[95] That the Jews were expelled from Rome is confirmed in Acts 18:2, where it is stated that Claudius had ordered all the Jews to leave Rome. In his commentary on the Book of Acts, F.F. Bruce dates the expulsion of the Jews to 49 C.E.[96], agreeing with Orosius, the 5th century church historian.[97]

There is little doubt that Jesus actually spoke the words, *Give to Caesar what is Caesar's and to God what is God's*. Of all the sayings in Mark's gospel that the scholars of the Jesus Seminar considered to be authentic, they gave the highest score (0.82) to this pronouncement.[98] But the coin, RPC 4161, has revealed that Mark changed the context in which Jesus's words were spoken. Instead of the Jews seeking Jesus's support for a complaint against the Romans, he changed it into a trap by the Jews to catch Jesus and bring about his death. Why has Mark done this?

If it is accepted that Mark was writing for a Roman audience, then it is obvious that he would be trying to win them over to Christianity, and in his gospel he portrays the Romans in the best light. As the Jews were the antagonists of the early Church, not only in Jerusalem but also in Rome, they are portrayed in a bad

---

[95] Suetonius, Twelve Caesars, 202.
[96] Bruce, F.F., *The Book of the Acts*. Grand Rapids: Eerdmans, 1988, 347.
[97] Orosius, *History*, 7.6.15-16.
[98] Funk, Robert W. and the Jesus Seminar, *The Gospel of Mark: red letter edition*. Sonoma: Polebridge Press, 1991.

light. For the Roman audience, the fact that Augustus was divine was self-evident: he had been the all-powerful ruler who had brought peace and prosperity to his vast empire, and temples and cults everywhere attested to his divinity. For those Romans who were being won over to the new, Christian religion there would have been no clear-cut distinction between monotheism and polytheism. Their religious thinking would have been a mixture of reverence for the emperor, devotion to the various gods, and ideas about the new religion. Mark would have been aware of this and adjusted his strategy accordingly. So he avoided criticising the emperor, not because he was afraid of the possible consequences, but because he was sensitive to the attitude of his audience. This pro-Roman stance is evident elsewhere in his gospel, e.g. he has a Roman centurion standing at the foot of the cross and declaring, "Surely this man was the son of God!" (Mark 15:39) Actually Mark had no alternative, because to criticise the emperor was tantamount to being anti-Roman, and if early Christianity had been anti-Roman it would never have got off the ground. Like Paul, he realised that the great task ahead was to convert the Gentiles.

In changing the context in this way, Mark might have felt that he was doing nothing wrong, but as previously explained, the meaning of Jesus's words is affected by the context. There might have been simply a lack of knowledge on Mark's part as to the exact circumstances in which Jesus made his tax-coin pronouncement, but it seems unlikely that Mark would have forgotten the circumstances if he had ever heard the story. In fact, as previously mentioned, he might have taken notes when he was with Peter, or he might have had with him a sayings collection, something like an early version of the gospel of Thomas. But even in the *Gospel of Thomas* a brief outline of the context is given, indicating that the coin was the initiating factor in the incident. A context is rarely given for the sayings in the *Gospel of Thomas*, but Jesus's tax-coin pronouncement requires a coin and some mention of tax, because it does not make sense on its own. Give what to Caesar? Why? It is difficult to avoid the conclusion that Mark knew the circumstances of the tax-coin incident but deliberately changed the story for his own purposes.

How could Mark have written something so contrary to fact if there were people who knew the story and could have denounced the falsehood? The most plausible explanation is that he was writing in relative isolation. To understand where and when this might have been, one needs to have some knowledge of Mark's movements and the events of the time.

After Peter's miraculous escape from prison in Jerusalem during the reign of Herod Agrippa I (41-44 C.E.) he went to the house of Mary, Mark's mother. (Acts 12:12, 13) It is clear from this passage that Mark's family was well established in Jerusalem with a large house and servants. This suggests that they were in good standing with the Roman authorities. Moreover, Mark's name is a common Roman name. In Latin it is Marcus, as in the name of the Roman emperor, Marcus Aurelius. It is therefore reasonable to assume that Mark's family had Roman connections. The fact that Mark also had a Jewish name, John, suggests that one of his parents was Jewish, and as Mary (Miriam) is a Jewish name the possibility arises that Mark's father was Roman or had Roman connections. In Mark 7:3 he refers to 'the Jews' as if he were not one of them or was distancing himself from them.

Although the book of Acts simply states that after being in Mary's house, Peter "left for another place" (Acts 12:17), John Wenham argues that Peter went to Rome.[99] Rome would have been the most suitable place for Peter to go at this time because Agrippa's agents would have been searching for him in Judea and adjacent areas. He would have been conspicuous in any of the provincial towns, but Rome at this time had a population of about a million inhabitants with a large Jewish population and people came to Rome from all parts of the empire. Peter could easily have jumped onto one of the wheat ships that called at ports in the province of Syria on their return journey to Rome from Alexandria. But Peter was a fisherman who probably spoke only Aramaic. He would have needed someone to accompany him,

---

[99] Wenham, J.W., *Redating Matthew and Luke: a fresh assault on the Synoptic Problem*. London: Hodder & Stoughton, 1991, 146.

someone who could speak at least some Greek. The most likely person to have filled this role was Mark, who might also have been able to speak Latin. As the child of a wealthy man he would have been taught Greek at least.

Eusebius states quite clearly that Peter went to Rome during the reign of Claudius (41-54 C.E.).[100] So it is quite possible that Peter and Mark were together in Rome from about 42 until about 49 C.E., when two significant events occurred. The first was the expulsion of the Jews from Rome and the second was the holding of the Jerusalem Council,[101] which was attended by Peter, Paul and other church leaders. Peter and Mark would have left Rome before 49 C.E. Peter's whereabouts after the council are unknown, but it would have been unwise for him to return to Rome, and he might have gone to the region of Pontus.[102] With Mark's Roman connections it would not have been so dangerous for him to return to Rome, but in Acts 15:39 it is recorded that after the council he was with his cousin Barnabas in Cyprus. Allowing for this delay, Mark could have been back in Rome in the early 50s, and presumably he would then have been a member of the community

---

[100] Eusebius, *Ecclesiastical History,* Book 2, Chapter 14, Section 1. See also 2.17.1.
[101] The council described in Galatians 2 is probably the same as in Acts 15.
[102] The First Letter of Peter is addressed to Christians in Pontus and neighbouring areas, which suggests that he had been there for some time. A faction that followed Peter is mentioned in 1 Cor 1:12, written about 55 C.E., but on his return trip to Jerusalem in about 49 C.E. Peter could have stayed in Corinth for some weeks or months.

of new Gentile Christians in Rome. They would have pressed him to write down what Peter had been saying in the synagogues about Jesus.

Concerning Mark's gospel there is the statement of Papias, the bishop of Hierapolis, who wrote in about 120 C.E.

*And the Elder said this also: Mark, having become the interpreter of Peter, wrote down accurately all that he remembered of the things said and done by the Lord, but not however in order. For neither did he hear the Lord, nor did he follow Him, but afterwards, as I said, Peter, who adapted his teachings to the needs (of the hearers), but not as though he were drawing up a connected account of the Lord's oracles. So then Mark made no mistake in thus recording some things just as he remembered them, for he made it his one care to omit nothing that he had heard and to make no false statement therein.*[103]

This suggests that there had been criticism of Mark because his order of events was not correct and because he omitted some things that he had heard and inserted fictitious information. The tax-coin incident might have been an example of the latter category. Referring to Papias' statement, Vincent Taylor considers that the force with which he affirms that Mark 'made no mistake'

---

[103] Eusebius, History, 3.39.15. Translation by Vincent Taylor.

shows that he too feels it necessary to defend Mark against current criticism.[104]

According to Eusebius, Mark left Rome and went to Egypt.[105] This must have occurred before Paul wrote his letter to the Romans because he makes no mention of Mark.[106] This letter was probably written in about 57 C.E. So Mark would have been in Rome from about 50 to about 56 C.E., and he probably wrote his gospel early in this period, i.e. about 52 C.E. Eusebius and Jerome both state that Mark died in the eighth year of Nero's reign, i.e. 61 C.E., at Alexandria.[107]

There is a strong tradition that Peter was martyred in Rome sometime after the fire that occurred in 64 C.E. Nero blamed the Christians for the fire, and presumably Peter returned to Rome to be with them. The commonly held view is that Mark was with Peter during this time and that after Peter's death in about 67 C.E. he wrote down what he 'remembered' of Peter's teaching.[108] However, Clement of Alexandria (*c.* 150-215 C.E.) says that Peter

---

[104] Taylor, Vincent, *The Gospel according to St. Mark.* London: Macmillan, 1966, 2.
[105] Eusebius, History, 2.16.1.
[106] Unless Romans 16.17 refers to Mark and his faction, in which case 'the obstacles' might have included Mark's gospel. Paul did not get on with Mark (Acts 15.39).
[107] Eusebius, History, 2.24.1. Jerome, *de Vir. Ill.*, 8.
[108] Irenaeus, *c.* 180 C.E., says that Mark wrote 'the things preached by Peter' after Peter's 'exodus'. See *Adv. Haer.* iii. 1. 2. Also the prologue to the Latin version of Mark's gospel states that Mark wrote after Peter's death, but this prologue was probably written in the 4$^{th}$ century.

was alive when Mark was writing and that when he knew of it "he neither actively prevented nor encouraged the undertaking."[109] Concerning Clement's last remark, that Peter was indifferent, Adolf von Harnack considered that it "can only have been occasioned by an opinion concerning the book, similar to that reported by Papias and John the Presbyter; i.e. because of certain faults in the gospel it was considered incredible that the book could have received the approbation of St Peter."[110] Also it is difficult to imagine that Mark could have written such a pro-Roman gospel after he had just witnessed the cruel execution of Peter and seen the atrocious cruelty of the Roman soldiers towards his fellow Christians. Moreover, it is inconceivable that the unflattering picture of Peter, which is presented in Mark's gospel, could have been written within a few years of his martyrdom. It is much more reasonable to assume that Mark had left Rome before the Neronian persecution and that he had written his gospel at an earlier time (about 52 C.E.) when he felt at liberty to "interpret" the teaching of Peter for the Roman Gentiles in keeping with his own attitude, which was favourable to all things Roman and against the Jews who had been opposing the Christians not only in Rome but in Judea and elsewhere.

---

[109] Quoted by Eusebius, History, 6.14.6.
[110] Von Harnack, Adolf, *The Date of the Acts and of the Synoptic Gospels*. London: Williams & Norgate, 1911, 129.

That Mark's gospel had been the target of criticism might explain why it was 'neglected'[111] by the early Church. This is reflected in the fact that of all the papyrus fragments dated to before the 5th century there is only one from Mark compared with eight from Matthew and four from Luke.[112] The usual reason given for this 'neglect' of Mark's gospel is that much of it is in the gospels of Matthew and Luke.[113] But this is only obvious when the gospels are critically compared, and presumably Mark would have had the advantage of Peter's authority. It seems more likely that factional rivalry was the cause. According to Vincent Taylor, "In the earliest references it is not disguised that from a very early date the Gospel was not accorded an unqualified welcome and was criticised for its want of order."[114] Apparently there were still people, presumably Jews, who had first-hand knowledge of Jesus's ministry.

With regard to Mark's account being out of order, John Selby Spong, referring to the work of Michael Goulder, considers that "the first gospel was written under the domination and influence of

---

[111] Martin, R., *Mark: evangelist and theologian*. Grand Rapids: Zondervan, 1973, 30.
[112] Aland, K. and B., *The Text of the New Testament,* 2nd ed. Grand Rapids: Eerdmans, 1989, 85.
[113] Over 97% of Mark's words have a parallel in Matthew's gospel and over 88% in Luke's gospel.
[114] Taylor, Gospel, 8.

the Jewish liturgical calendar."[115] Concerning the 'organising principle' of Mark's account Spong writes, "The content of this gospel appears to have existed first as Christian preaching on the lections of the synagogue and as the Christian attempt to interpret Jesus in terms of the great festivals of the Jewish liturgical year."[116]

Thus a likely scenario for the formation of Mark's gospel is as follows. Persecution of Christians was severe when Agrippa I was king of Judea from 41 to 44 C.E. He killed James, one of Jesus's disciples, and imprisoned Peter. Peter escaped in about 42 C.E. and went to Rome, accompanied by Mark who had Roman connections. Unlike Paul, Peter remained focused on telling Jews about Jesus and when he arrived in Rome he became involved with the Jews there and their synagogue worship. After a few years some of the Jews began to oppose Peter and violent disturbances occurred, causing Claudius to expel the Jews in 49 C.E. The Gentile Christians were not expelled. Peter attended the Council of Jerusalem in 49 C.E. and afterwards went to remote parts of Asia Minor. So he would have been in Rome from 42 to 49 C.E. After the council Mark went with Barnabas to Cyprus, but aware of the council's endorsement of the mission to the Gentiles, he returned to Rome where he wrote his pro-Roman, anti-Jewish account. In

---

[115] Spong, J.S., *Liberating the Gospels*. San Francisco: Harper, 1997, 77.
[116] Spong, Liberating, 86.

other centres, such as Ephesus, Mark was criticised for introducing fictitious material and because the account was not 'in order'. This scenario would explain how the story of a group of Jews from Antioch showing a tetradrachm of Antioch to Jesus for his advice, was changed to Jesus asking for a denarius in the presence of Jews who were trying to trap and kill him.

The light shone on the tax-coin incident by RPC 4161 reveals the Jewishness of Jesus. The group of leading Jews from Antioch would hardly have consulted him if he had been a type of Greek Cynic philosopher. Nor would they have consulted him if he was perceived as more Hellenistic than Jewish. The Greeks particularly liked to portray their gods in pictures and statuary, while such images were forbidden to the Jews. According to Genesis 1:27, humankind was made in the image of God, and that image belonged to God. In consulting Jesus about the tax-coin matter the Jews assumed that he was well qualified to advise on such matters.

Although Matthew and Luke relied heavily on Mark's gospel when writing their own there would have been some input from other sources and from the oral tradition. But the insight provided by RPC 4161 allows for a fresh appraisal of the way the synoptic gospels were formed. The idea of a long period during which a 'fluid' oral tradition was moulded and transformed by various Christian communities is a misconception. Virtually the whole process was brief and written.[117] Any rearranging of material according to function was done by Peter during his years of teaching in and outside the synagogues of Rome before 49 C.E. and by Mark when he recorded Peter's teaching for his Roman audience. Peter was a witness to what Jesus said and did, and after only 22 years from the time of Jesus's death, Mark wrote what he remembered of Peter's teaching in the light of his own attitude and situation. From then on, although Matthew and Luke made changes in accordance with their own perceptions, the essentials of the story as presented in the synoptic gospels were fixed.

The argument presented in this paper concerning the identity of the Tribute Penny[118] and the writing of Mark's gospel is, of course, only a hypothesis. A number of assumptions were made, e.g. that the person who wrote the gospel is the 'Mark' who accompanied Barnabas to Cyprus, and there was a degree of speculation. However, as in scientific studies, theories should be put forward and considered by the relevant scholars until they are proved to be untenable. It was in this spirit that the present paper was written.

---

[117] The gospel was spread by the written word being communicated to people, not by people remembering events and sayings, telling others about them, and then someone collecting the information to write a gospel.

[118] The case for RPC 4161 being the Tribute Penny has previously been presented by the author in an article entitled 'The Actual Tribute Penny' in the *Journal of the Numismatic Association of Australia*, Vol. 10, 1999, pp. 3-13, and in an article entitled 'The Actual Tribute Penny' in the *Journal of the Society for Ancient Numismatics*, Vol. XXI, 2002, pp. 26-30.

The Jews show a coin to Jesus in the Temple (1752 copperplate engraving).

# Afterword

Having thoroughly investigated the matter, there is no doubt that Mark's gospel did not end with 'for they were afraid.' As the reconstruction showed, it continued into an important final section, the key points of which were magnified by Luke in his gospel. Similarly the beginning is not the beginning that Mark wrote, as the reconstruction showed. The original beginning and ending were removed by a faction of early Christians who objected to what Mark wrote. It is obvious that this pro-Peter group did not want Mary Magdalene and those with her to be recognised and given a position of primacy. Also they objected to what Mark wrote about Jesus's origins. They were Gentiles who expected their Jesus to have a miraculous origin like Hercules and the other great figures of their world. They were a powerful group able to influence the scriptures of early Christianity, and they were almost certainly in Rome at the centre of the empire. The issues raised by this investigation are serious matters of great importance to modern Christians. They need to be carefully considered by everyone.

# More reviews of the Ending of Mark's Gospel

Peter Lewis develops a fascinating theory that deals with the puzzling end of the Gospel according to Mark. Part of the proposal is that the original first page was also removed. Peter's well-developed argument carries important implications for some of the debates that are concerning the church at this time. He proposes a way to push through the gender and sexuality wars that so hold back the church's proclamation of the God of Love.
*The Very Reverend Dr Peter Catt, Dean of Brisbane, St John's Anglican Cathedral.*

\* \* \*

In regard to the article about the ending of Mark's gospel, I think your ideas are very well thought out, and ought to be published.
*Reverend Richard Plant. Yorkshire, England. Author of 'Greek Coin Types and their Identification' (1979), 'Greek, Semitic Asiatic Coins and how to read them' (revised edition, 2013), etc.*

\* \* \*

There are many mysteries around the creation and early transmission of the Gospel according to Mark, the oldest of the gospels in the New Testament. Peter Lewis invites his readers on a journey to explore how this gospel lost not only its original final page but perhaps also its original opening scenes. I think the collection of essays in this little volume offer thoughtful people a helpful insight into the origins of the New Testament and the deeper dynamics of our faith in today's world.

*Dr Gregory C. Jenks, Dean of Grafton and Director of the Centre for Coins, Culture and Religious History. Author of 'Jesus Then and Jesus Now' (2014) and 'The Once and Future Bible' (2011). https://cccrh.org*

\* \* \*

Peter Lewis has written a stimulating study that suggests new ways of understanding Mark's gospel. Over the years scholars have been intrigued by the wording of both the beginning and the ending of this gospel. Peter's book offers the reader several pathways into this most interesting gospel territory.

*Dr Ray Barraclough. For some years Ray lectured in biblical studies in both Jerusalem and Brisbane. He is currently Treasurer of A Progressive Christian Voice (Australia) Inc [APCVA].*

\* \* \*

Intrigued by the mention of a particular coin in the wrong place at the wrong time, numismatist and biblical scholar Dr Peter E. Lewis decides to investigate. In a true spirit of discovery, he ends up re-examining the entire gospel of St Mark, particularly its abrupt beginning and ending, which have been the subject of a persistent debate among scholars for centuries. His quest for the truth with no vested interest in the outcome is rewarded by an inspired solution, which is not only logical but also surprisingly empowering to women. This methodically researched, meticulously referenced and well-reasoned book suggests that women have been denied their rightful place in the church, and the humanity of Jesus should be given more recognition. A must-read for Christians and non-Christians alike.

*Dr James Coates. Brisbane, Queensland.*

\* \* \*

An interpreter of the gospel of Mark always has a problem with its ending. It reads as if the last sentence has been cut in half. At some later times a Shorter Ending and a Longer Ending have tried to fill the gap – without great success. Peter Lewis, a retired medical specialist who also has qualifications in biblical studies, offers a unique solution. Somebody tore off the last page of the Markan codex for whatever reason. If so, the connected front page would also have been torn off! Lewis takes up the tantalising questions: who might have desecrated the early codex? Why? And what is the result for generations of later Christians? In lucid prose, Lewis provides a credible solution. This is a very attractive book, both for specialist and general enquirer.

*Robert Crotty, Emeritus Professor of Religion and Education, University of South Australia.*

\* \* \*

www.ingramcontent.com/pod-product-compliance
Lightning Source LLC
Chambersburg PA
CBHW071518080526
44588CB00011B/1475